# *Meeting the Challenge*

## Special Education Tools
that Work for All Kids

**by Patti Ralabate**
NEA Professional Library

**Printing History**

First Printing: June 2002

Note: The opinions in this publication should not be construed as representing the policy or position of the National Education Association. Materials published by the NEA Professional Library are intended to be discussion documents for educators who are concerned with specialized interests of the profession.

This book is printed on acid-free paper.

ACID FREE
∞

**Library of Congress Cataloging-in-Publication Data**

Ralabate, Patti.
    Meeting the challenge: special education tools that work for all kids / by Patti Ralabate.
        p. cm.
    "An NEA Professional Library publication."
    Includes bibliographical references.
    ISBN 0-8106-2022-7
1. Children with disabilities—Education—United States—Handbooks, manuals, etc. 2. Individualized education programs—United States—Handbooks, manuals, etc. 3. Special education—United States—Handbooks, manuals, etc. I. Title.

LC4031 .R37 2002
379.9'0973—dc21

                                                                        2002072806

# Table of Contents

# Acknowledgements

More than a quarter century of teaching students with a variety of needs in the public schools went into the development of this book. During these many years, scores of exceptional educators, parents, and students added to my skills and opened my eyes to their insights.

In particular, I want to acknowledge the support of Stephanie Fanjul and the assistance of Joyce Emmett, Sharon Schultz, Marcie Dianda, Barbara Kapinus, Pam Matthews, Fran Harris, Penny Kotterman, and Richard Liston. Many of the book's strategies and ideas resulted from working with truly extraordinary team members over the last 25 years, specifically Karen Allen, Anne Benninghof, Margie Blansfield, Cathy Buhrman, Janet Butera, Lenore Chiappetta, Priscilla Eller, Peggy Fielding, Linda Foege, Donna Hart, Karen Hores, Linda La Boy,

Anna Lopes, Marilyn Maneri, Linda Moritz, Joan Nash, Vonnie Neufeld, Meghan Phelan, Marie Plunkett, Marita Repole, Liz Smith, Miriam Stein, Fran Tyluki, and the members of the NEA IDEA Special Education Resource Cadre. Above all, I learned the most from my beloved students, especially Adam, Bobby, Brian, Bridget, Christina, Danny, Edward, Eric, Fernando, James, Kevin, Lawrence, Michael, Nabila, Nathan, Noah, Rocky, Sebastian, Sierra, Skylar, Vishnu, and William.

Text becomes a book through the expertise of numerous people. I thank Christian Lopez for the beautiful cover, Hallie Logan Shell for the superb layout, and Lauren Fischer for the vast list of resources.

However, this book would not have been possible without the incredible talents of my editor, Sabrina Holcomb, and the enduring love and encouragement of my husband Sam and my daughter Kelly.

# Introduction

*"Let us put our minds together and see what life we can make*

*for our children."*

Sitting Bull, Lakota Sioux

Over the last quarter-century, educators and parents have earnestly "put their minds together" to try to develop good education programs and services for students who show academic and behavioral difficulties. You could reasonably presume that in the years since the first federal special education law was passed in 1975, schools have perfected the art of educating students with special needs. In a few places, this is true.

In many schools across the country, however, efforts to educate students with special needs are barely adequate. Scores of educators report they are weighted down with burdensome paperwork, confused by changing requirements, upset by increasing demands, stymied by a lack of supports, and frustrated by an ever-growing number of students with academic and behavioral problems.

Despite these challenges, several shining stars of success and promising practices exist. Various schools are using approaches that make the task of teaching struggling students

and students with disabilities a productive and rewarding endeavor. These approaches include a classroom-oriented focus, effective collaborative teams, educationally relevant student expectations, and efficient communication strategies among team members and parents.

## Who Can Use This Book

When a student is struggling in your classroom, you need resources.

Over the last 25 years, we've discovered that most of the strategies used with students who have disabilities are great teaching techniques to use with other students who have academic or behavior difficulties. *Meeting the Challenge* was written with this thought in mind. General education teachers can use many of the strategies in this book with any students who are struggling in their classrooms.

Special education teachers and related service personnel will also find the materials in this book convenient and valuable. Although special educators are already familiar with some of the best practices described in this book, they still seek resources in particular areas—such as working on collaborative teams, communicating effectively with parents, and dealing with student behavior.

For the most part, the ideas in this book can be used whether your student is disabled and has an Individualized Education Program (IEP) or not. *Meeting the Challenge* is filled with ideas and suggestions that can help make your job easier and your teaching more effective. Each chapter discusses a topic of concern to educators in both general education and special education areas. And for clarification, special terms are italicized when they are first introduced and are defined in the Glossary.

Teachers should use this book as a toolkit. Throughout the book, you'll find illustrations and explanations of practical, timesaving strategies and worksheets. The Appendix contains perforated forms you can tear out and copy, or adapt and use as needed. The forms are "blank" formats of the worksheets, planning guides, checklists, assessment forms, and other resources introduced in the book.

The main purposes of this book are to help you by: 1) providing suggestions about strategies that work, 2) sharing resources to address your most troubling challenges, and 3) offering handy worksheets that can reduce some of your paperwork burden.

## How We Got Here

Educators and parents had to rethink how to best teach students with disabilities after the Individuals with Disabilities Education Act

(IDEA) was reauthorized by Congress in 1997. A fundamental assumption in IDEA '97—that students with disabilities should have access to the general education curriculum—caused a major shift in emphasis across the country.

Now, programs for students with disabilities must align with the state or local standards that apply to all students. Why? The answer requires an understanding of the bigger context affecting public education over the last 20 years.

The national focus on improving education, commonly referred to as the "Standards-Based Reform Movement," began after the publication of *A Nation at Risk,* a report by the United States Department of Education's National Commission on Excellence in Education, in 1983. While the initial discussions did not speak specifically to the needs of students with disabilities, many of the movement's underlying assumptions had a dramatic impact on their education. The notion that all students can learn if schools provide challenging curriculum and instruction was one of the most influential and controversial ideas.

After the 1989 National Education Summit, policymakers and educational leaders from all over the country pushed states to develop standards defining high expectations for all students. Forty-nine states now have academic standards that pertain to all students, including those with disabilities.

Many national leaders felt that the expectations for students with disabilities were not commensurate with those for nondisabled students. Some believed that students who were academically behind were actually held to lower standards and instructed in a "watered-down" curriculum. When Congress passed IDEA '97, lawmakers decided it was time to include students with disabilities in the standards-based reform movement. This is one of the reasons why IDEA '97 stated that students with disabilities must have access to, participate in, and progress in the general education curriculum.

In addition, IDEA '97 stated that students with disabilities must be included in state- and district-wide assessments. Lawmakers wanted to measure whether or not students with disabilities were achieving at higher levels and how well they were progressing in the general education curriculum.

## What's Ahead

This book is being published as work on the reauthorization of IDEA begins. Congress will try to address lingering problems as they examine the effects of IDEA '97. Due to the timing of this book, when we mention certain requirements of IDEA, we are referring to the provisions of IDEA '97. If necessary, a revised edition will be published after reauthorization is completed.

Lawmakers made considerable modifications to programs for struggling students, such as

Title I, when the Elementary and Secondary Education Act (ESEA) was signed into law on January 8, 2002, as "H.R. 1, No Child Left Behind Act of 2001." While it's hard to predict what changes may be made in the federal special education law, one thing is a sure bet: you'll continue to have students in your classroom who have special needs, and your desire for suggestions and resources to meet the challenge of educating your students will persist.

This book was written as a freestanding reference tool for anyone involved in educating students with academic or behavior difficulties. In particular, the following chapters will help you address six critical areas:

1. Evaluating struggling students using classroom-based assessments.

2. Observing behavior and positively addressing behavioral challenges.

3. Using a collaborative team process.

4. Developing educationally relevant student expectations.

5. Providing accommodations and modifications.

6. Communicating effectively with parents.

# How To Assess Struggling Students

*"My heart is singing for joy this morning. A miracle has happened!*

*The light of understanding has shone upon my little pupil's mind, and*

*behold, all things are changed!"*

Annie Sullivan

Every teacher has a reason why he or she chose to enter the teaching profession. For many, the notion of causing the "light of understanding" to shine upon a student's face is reason enough. When a student in your classroom struggles and that "light of understanding" dims despite your best teaching efforts, it can be enormously frustrating for both of you.

Teachers naturally reach out for resources to help struggling students. Sometimes that means using alternative teaching strategies in the classroom. Sometimes it means referring students for an evaluation to find out if they qualify for *special education* services. No matter which road you ultimately take, the first thing you need to do is identify your students' needs.

This chapter will suggest ways you can draw on what you know about your students' classroom performance to assess their skills, define their needs, and choose interventions that will help them succeed.

## The First Step in Helping Your Student

For a long time, it seemed the only way you could help a struggling student was to refer him or her for a special education evaluation. The general education classroom teacher might make the initial referral but have little involvement after that. Things have changed.

The classroom teacher is now expected to gather data that will help determine what interventions to use with a student. The teacher assesses a student's skills and monitors

## Chapter 1

**Tool 1.1**
Analytic Rubric

**Tool 1.2**
Holistic Rubric

**Tool 1.3**
Skills Checklist

**Tool 1.4**
Intervention Progress Sheet

**Additional tools in Appendix**

his or her progress on an ongoing basis in the classroom. An early intervention team often helps the teacher gather this information. This is a very important first step in helping a struggling student.

## The Early Intervention Team

No educator, no matter how experienced or skilled, is able to meet all the unique instructional needs of every child without the assistance of colleagues. Whether you're instructing a student who is struggling, or a student with a disability who has an *Individualized Education Program (IEP)*, you'll need to work with a team, but the teams will differ throughout different stages of the process. Many schools now have early intervention teams that meet with classroom teachers to provide assistance for students who are demonstrating problems in the classroom.

The early intervention team often includes related services personnel (e.g., school psychologist, guidance counselor, social worker, or speech-language pathologist) and remedial or instructional resource staff (e.g., reading specialist, math specialist, or English-as-a-second language teacher). An effective team model would also include several general education classroom teachers, the school nurse, and the principal.

The team in your school may go by a different name: early intervention team, pre-referral team, child study team, student assistance team, teacher support team, etc. No matter what the team is called, it usually has two purposes: 1) to offer suggestions for your students who are having academic or behavioral problems (general education alternative strategies) and 2) to help you analyze and record your observations and assessment data for the documentation that's needed to initiate a special education referral, if necessary.

Even if an early intervention team doesn't presently exist in your school, you can call on colleagues in your school or district to offer suggestions for alternative teaching strategies or, if needed, to put together the documentation for a special education referral.

### The Intervention Team Process

There is no one formula for how early intervention teams work. Different states and schools use varying procedures. An effective team relies heavily on gathering data in the initial stages. Then, using a collaborative problem-solving process, the team provides opportunities for teachers to brainstorm possible intervention strategies with other teachers. Always, the key decision maker remains the classroom teacher. She or he determines which data are useful and which instructional strategies to use in the classroom. Many states (e.g., Arkansas, California, Connecticut, Florida, Hawaii, Indiana, Kentucky, Maryland) use an early intervention team process that includes the following steps:

**Gather data.** Make observations and gather data about your student's skills and levels of performance. *(What has your student learned? How does she/he learn?)*

**Analyze.** Study your data to identify a focused area or skill for improvement. *(What skill does your student need to learn?)*

**Determine an objective.** Develop a specific measurable objective. *(What should your student be doing in a few weeks or a month?)*

**Consider alternative strategies.** Brainstorm to generate alternative strategies and interventions. *(What strategies can you use in the classroom to help your student learn?)*

**Write an action plan.** Develop and implement an intervention plan. *(Which strategy is feasible and likely to succeed? Who does what when?)*

**Check progress.** Monitor progress and evaluate the success of the intervention. *(Is the plan working? Has your student reached the objective?)*

# Classroom-Based Assessments

Assessment actually refers to a process of collecting information on a student. It's far more comprehensive than simply giving one standardized test. That's why *classroom-based assessments (CBAs)* are typically the most authentic student data available because they're based on your classroom and curriculum expectations. They include daily and weekly quizzes, tests, checklists, rating scales, rubrics, portfolios, and classroom observations. In simple order, you teach a lesson, then you evaluate whether or not your students learned it.

When you're evaluating student behavior rather than academic performance, you'll rely on *observation-based assessments (OBAs)* rather than classroom-based assessments. Further discussion of OBAs appears in Chapter 2. For the purposes of this section of the book, we'll explore academic CBA strategies.

Five questions to consider while doing classroom-based assessments are:

1. What information have I taught?

2. What are my expectations for student learning at this point?

3. What does this student know?

4. What can this student do?

5. When this student can't do something, what does he or she do instead?

## Observation

The most direct way to collect information on students' skills is to watch them. Unobtrusive classroom observations are authentic measures for many skill areas that are not easily "tested." For example, social interaction skills, self-confidence, and group participation abilities are all areas that are demonstrated daily and can be readily observed.

## Baseline Data

Before you start any new interventions or alternative strategies, make initial observations and assessments of your student's ability to do the targeted skill or task. This is your *baseline data.* You're measuring what your student knows or is able to do without extra help.

## Designing Assessments

As you design your classroom-based assessments, consider these five questions:

1. **Are my assessments specific?** Focus the scope of your observations and assessments on a specific skill or skill set.

Descriptions such as "She can't read anything" or "He never pays attention" may be accurate reflections of your frustrations but are meaningless for assessment purposes. You need to determine a specific task you can observe and measure using a classroom-based assessment.

2. **Are my assessments fair?** Asking your student to respond to test items about curriculum content that hasn't been taught isn't fair. Assessments must be aligned with curriculum, grade, and age-level expectations. All assessments must be linguistically and culturally nonbiased.

3. **Are my assessments valid?** In other words, are they measuring the intended skill or area of knowledge? If you wanted to assess your student's fluency of reading, you wouldn't have him or her read a list of sight words. To get a valid assessment of reading fluency, you would ask your student to read a timed passage and then calculate the number of words read per minute. *(See the Calculating Reading Rate sidebar on page 16.)*

4. **Are my assessments comprehensive?** Sometimes, you need to determine your student's ability in several distinct but linked skill areas, such as written

## CALCULATING READING RATE

Reading Rate measures the fluency and speed of a student's oral or silent reading in words per minute (WPM). It evaluates how rapidly a student can recognize words in a reading passage. Reading rate is only one component of a complete reading assessment and should be used with other measures to get a complete assessment of a student's reading level.

### Procedures:

**Method A:** Time your student reading a passage for one minute. Stop after one minute and then record how many words he/she read in the one-minute period.

**Method B:** Have your student read an entire passage and note how long it took, then calculate the reading rate using this formula:

1. Convert the time into seconds. (e.g., 1 minute and 15 seconds = 75 seconds).

2. Divide the number of seconds by the number of words in the passage.

Multiply the resulting number by 60 to calculate the reading rate as words read per minute.

language skills. In these instances, be sure to evaluate your student's skills with an assessment procedure that's as comprehensive as possible. Many teachers use rubrics because they provide a scoring scheme that evaluates the quality and proficiency of student work in descriptive terms. An analytic rubric, rating scale, or skills checklist may give you more valuable information than a generic holistic rubric. *(See Tools 1, 2, and 3—a sample Analytic Rubric, Holistic Rubric, and Skills Checklist—on pages 18, 19, and 20.)*

5. **Are my assessments reliable?** To get a reliable measurement, you must present information in a consistent manner. This way you can be sure you're assessing the same skill every time. For example, if you're assessing your student's ability to identify 10 letters of the alphabet out of order, then you must ask him or her to identify the same 10 letters presented in random order every time.

## Guidelines for Data Analysis

After you collect the data about your student's performance, you're ready to analyze it. Keep these guidelines in mind:

**Visually represent your data.** It's amazing how a series of scores can look like paint drippings when listed on a sheet of paper but turn into a clearly defined picture of your student's skill levels when presented on a chart or graph. Line and bar graphs are particularly effective ways to present a series of percentages.

**Look for obvious gaps.** Analytic rubrics and checklists can help you identify gaps in student learning. If earlier gaps in learning are evident, you may want to provide direct instruction in those prerequisite areas before moving on.

**Look for patterns.** Different data measuring the same skill area over several days or weeks can help you see certain weaknesses within that area. For example, if your student does well at the end of one week but not at the beginning of the following week, the problem may be difficulty with content retention. When your student's performance deteriorates after a series of trials or a few days, it may mean that he or she is fatigued or is no longer motivated.

**Look for gains.** How long it takes for your student to learn a skill (learning rate) can sometimes be even more valuable information than what he or she knows or doesn't know. For example, if a student has limited school experience and makes learning gains on a CBA over several days, that can be considered a significant gain for that student.

**Recognize competence.** Mastery is usually defined as 80-90 percent accuracy over three to five consecutive trials. While there are some instances when we expect 100 percent performance (e.g., looking carefully before we cross a busy street), our expectations need to be reasonable.

# Analytic Rubric of Prewriting Skills

Analytic rubrics yield good diagnostic information because they provide details about your student's strengths and those areas that need improvement. An analytic rubric of prewritten language skills might include several descriptors under different traits, such as idea generation, organization, audience, purpose, form, and format. This particular rubric is designed so that students can use it as a self-evaluation tool.

## Task:

Now that you've finished your writing assignment, take a look at the chart below and find which prewriting skills you used.

|  | Novice | Developing | Expected | Mastery |
|---|---|---|---|---|
| **Idea Generation** | I thought of one idea and started writing. | I thought of a few ideas and then chose one. | I thought of many ideas and then chose one. | I thought of several ideas, solicited ideas from others, and then chose one. |
| **Organization of Ideas** | I began writing without a plan. | I jotted a few notes but did not use a graphic organizer. | I used a graphic organizer to develop a detailed plan. | I used a detailed graphic organizer that included my ideas as well as suggestions from others. |
| **Consideration of Audience and Purpose** | I did not identify an audience or a purpose. | I identified an audience and purpose but did not write with them in mind. | I wrote with my audience and purpose in mind. | I gathered additional information about my audience and/or purpose before I began writing. |
| **Writing Form and Format** | I selected neither the appropriate form nor format. | I selected either the appropriate form or format. | I selected both the appropriate form and format. | After considering possible alternatives, I selected the most appropriate form and format. |

Developed by Lori Windler, East Tipp Middle School, Lafayette, IN, March 2002

# Holistic Rubric of Expository Written Language

Holistic rubrics list expected skills at sequenced points along a continuum of performance levels and then yield one total score. Holistic rubrics are most appropriate for grading or making summative judgments about student work.

## Procedure:

Determine which descriptors and corresponding heading best applies to your student's work. Your student's score is 0, 1, 2, or 3.

**Score: 3**      **Meets Expectations**

Work is focused and fully developed without irrelevant information.

Ideas are sequenced and appropriately supported.

Effective transitions are used throughout.

Correct grammar, capitalization, and spelling are used throughout.

**Score: 2**      **Adequate**

There are minimal distractions in flow of thought.

Some support is provided for ideas, but they are not clearly explained.

Basic transitions are used.

There are some errors in mechanics (grammar, capitalization, spelling).

**Score: 1**      **Needs Improvement**

There are numerous distractions in flow of thought.

The format is rambling and poorly organized.

Support is insufficient, irrelevant, or ambiguous.

Transitions are inadequate.

There are numerous errors in mechanics.

**Score: 0**      **Inadequate**

There appears to be no organization of thought or content.

Sentences are difficult to read and understand.

**Student Score:** _____

# Checklist for Expository Written Language Skills

Checklists are lists of traits within skill areas. They generally provide a quick measure of a student's strengths or skill levels in defined areas. The following checklist is for expository written language skills. Evaluate each of the areas independently and add them together for a total score. Given successively over time, a checklist can provide incremental views of a student's learning.

## Procedure:

Under each trait listed below, check all that apply to your student's writing. Add the total number of items checked and enter the total on the line at the bottom. If all the descriptors under each trait are present, the total score is 24.

**Focus**
___ topic is clearly addressed/established
___ topic is carefully introduced at the beginning with at least 3 support statements
___ topic remains clear throughout

**Development**
___ focus is on topic without irrelevant information
___ ideas are fully developed
___ ideas/theme is unique/creative
___ sustains reader interest

**Organization**
___ ideas are sequenced
___ includes clear beginning, middle, and end
___ uses a summary statement
___ conclusion is logical

**Elaboration**
___ uses interesting examples and details
___ uses adjectives and adverbs to enhance descriptions
___ expresses personal thoughts/feelings
___ word choice is accurate/vivid
___ uses descriptive phrases and clauses
___ includes analogies

**Structure and Writing Mechanics**
___ uses varying patterns and sentence length
___ includes simple, compound, and complex sentence structure
___ uses paragraphing appropriately (2+ sentences with topic sentence)
___ includes transition words smoothly to link sentences/paragraphs
___ uses subject/verb agreement in sentences
___ uses correct capitalization and punctuation
___ spells words correctly

**SCORE** _____ / __24__

## Developing Your Intervention Plan

By now, you should have enough information to decide what your student's objective will be.

### Choosing the Objective

Choose an objective that addresses what you think is the main problem. Ask this question: *If I can change only one thing, what will make the biggest difference for my student?*

When writing your specific objective, be careful to focus on the problem behavior or skill, not what you believe is causing it. A student's behavior can be so complex and confusing, it's hard to know exactly why the problem exists. Consider Allyson's story below.

## ALLYSON'S STORY

Allyson never handed in classroom assignments. Her baseline for work completion was zero. Her teacher didn't know if Allyson lacked motivation to complete her work, didn't understand assignments, was unwilling to comply with classroom expectations, or was so distracted or disorganized that she started work but never finished it. Even though work completion was the problem, the reason remained elusive. The teacher chose daily work completion as the specific objective for Allyson. He hoped that by focusing on the problem, the reason(s) for the problem might become more obvious.

A sample objective for Allyson could be: *Within five weeks, given only one verbal reminder per day, Allyson will complete daily written assignments on four out of five days with 90 percent accuracy.*

Think about these questions as you design your specific objective:

1. What specific task or skill do I want my student to achieve? *(e.g., Allyson will complete daily written assignments.)*

2. What conditions and extra help should be in place? *(e.g., one verbal reminder per day)*

3. How am I going to measure the objective? *(e.g., Work will be placed in the "finished" basket, completed with at least 90 percent accuracy.)*

4. What level of competence do I expect? *(e.g., Allyson will complete her assignments four out of five days.)*

5. How long should it take before I move on to a new objective or decide the intervention isn't working? *(e.g., within five weeks)*

### Choosing Alternative Strategies

Which intervention strategy you choose is critical. Make sure you look at many options before you decide. If you've hit a point of frustration, you may feel you've tried every strategy there is without success. Your school's early intervention team can help you brainstorm a variety of different intervention strategies. Keep an open mind to their suggestions.

There are numerous books and online resources about alternative strategies. Some districts make lists of alternative strategies available to classroom teachers. *(See the Intervention Strategies Menu in the Appendix.)*

## Implementing the Plan

Review a number of alternative strategies, then choose one or two that are the most "doable" and develop your intervention plan. While you're implementing the intervention plan, you may continue to consult with your school's early intervention team, especially if you have questions or problems. Consider the following elements for your student's intervention plan:

**Responsibility.** Identify who is responsible for what.

**Data collection.** Once you choose and introduce a strategy, keep track of your student's performance toward the objective.

**Documentation.** Consistently note your student's performance and record it. *(Use a graph or progress sheet like Tool 1.4, the Intervention Progress Sheet, on page 23.)* If you graph your data, it will be easier to analyze.

**Timeframe.** Normally, you need at least two or three weeks of data before you can make judgments about whether the plan is working.

## Reviewing Progress

After you implement the intervention plan for the designated time period, the key question to ask is: *Has the objective been achieved?* Your data will tell you the answer.

If your student achieves the objective, you have a few options: 1) maintain the intervention because it's working, 2) move on to another objective that is now more pressing, or 3) end the intervention because the problem is resolved. It's a good idea to continue to monitor your student's progress for a while to make sure his or her performance stabilizes.

## ANOTHER LOOK

**Let's take another look at Allyson's situation.** Allyson's teacher used an Intervention Progress Sheet to graph her data *(See Tool 1.4)*. Her baseline data is represented on the graph by the first three days (i.e., 0 percent for 10/1, 10/2, 10/3). The intervention the teacher chose was to present Allyson with one assignment at a time and to give her a sticker on a chart each time she handed in a completed assignment. He introduced the intervention on October 4. By the next day, October 5, Allyson began to respond by handing in two assignments (40 percent = work completion). Approximately 30 percent of the work she handed in was accurate (30 percent = accuracy). Allyson's teacher continued with this intervention because it seemed to be helping. By the end of the next week, Allyson handed in all five assignments with 100 percent accuracy. Her performance dropped off slightly during the next week, but she continued to complete more work than she had previously. Within three weeks, Allyson was consistently handing in all five assignments and they were 90 percent accurate.

# Intervention Progress Sheet

**Student:** Allyson B.  **Grade:** 4

**Teacher:** Mr. Jones  **Case Partner** M. Smith

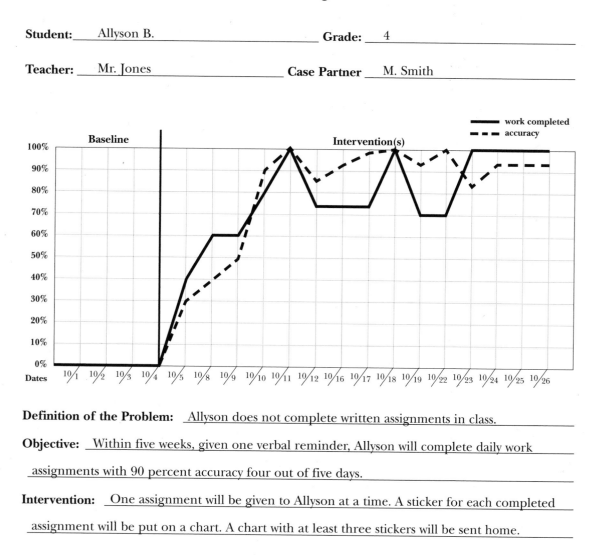

**Definition of the Problem:** Allyson does not complete written assignments in class.

**Objective:** Within five weeks, given one verbal reminder, Allyson will complete daily work assignments with 90 percent accuracy four out of five days.

**Intervention:** One assignment will be given to Allyson at a time. A sticker for each completed assignment will be put on a chart. A chart with at least three stickers will be sent home.

If your student doesn't achieve the objective and you see little to no progress, all this work is still valuable! You now know far more about what your student knows and how he or she learns than you did before. In addition, the data you've collected can help you either 1) choose a different intervention or 2) document a referral for a special education evaluation.

## Special Education Referral

If your initial interventions aren't successful, you may decide to refer a student for a special education evaluation. The *Individuals with Disabilities Education Act (IDEA)* said that a special education evaluation should include classroom-based assessments made by the teacher and assessment data from specialists. Together, this information helps to define the student's *present levels of performance* for the IEP team.

### Why Do All This?

Conferring with a child study team, gathering data, and coming up with an intervention plan may seem like more work up front, but it will make your life a lot easier in the long run. In addition to helping you with a struggling student, the early intervention team process gives you the tools you need to become a better teacher. Using these techniques, you'll be able to identify learning needs in your classroom and design appropriate instruction. In the long run, your teaching will be more successful and your job more manageable.

# 2 Students with Challenging Behavior

*"We live in a decadent age. Young people no longer respect their parents.*

*They are rude and impatient. They inhabit taverns and have no self-control."*

Inscription on 6,000-year-old Egyptian tomb

We've been concerned about the behavior of our children since civilization began. Children misbehave sometimes. As educators, we know this. We know, too, that some students' conduct stands out as unusual, more aggressive, or more challenging than others. When students have behavioral difficulties of this magnitude, it can affect their learning and the learning of others. It can frustrate you, other members of your instructional team, and parents.

This chapter suggests ways to observe a student's behavior in your classroom. We'll discuss how to write a Behavior Intervention Plan (BIP) for any student who needs one. Since your classroom is a part of the school community, we'll also discuss classroom and school-wide behavioral support strategies that can help you cultivate a positive learning environment for all students.

## Students Without IEPs

If you have students who show disruptive behavior or other kinds of actions that interfere with their learning, you may not know where to start. Working with the early intervention team in your school should be your first step. The team can help you develop classroom interventions to address students' difficult behaviors. With the intervention team's assistance, you can nip emerging problems in the bud before they become chronic discipline issues.

### Chapter 2 Toolkit

**Tool 2.1**
Observable Positive and Negative Behaviors Chart

**Tool 2.2**
Behavior Observation Form

**Tool 2.3**
Behavior Intervention Plan

**Tool 2.4**
Behavior Observation Tally Sheet

**Tool 2.5**
Possible Data Collection Methods

Sometimes teachers subdue a student's disruptive behavior during the intervention process only to find that underlying academic problems are causing the student to act out. In this case, you and the team can then change the focus of your assessments and interventions to address your student's academic deficits. The work you did up to this point is not lost effort. By first resolving behavioral concerns, you've helped to clarify and document your student's true needs.

## Students with IEPs

Some students with disabilities have mild to severe behavior difficulties that may or may not be related to their disabilities. Successfully dealing with their behavior in your classroom can be challenging for everyone on your instructional team.

IDEA required that the IEP team consider strategies, including positive behavioral supports, to address behavior that impedes a student's learning or that of others. We recommend that the IEP team anticipate behavioral episodes if your student has chronic behavior difficulties. By conducting a Functional Behavioral Assessment and developing a Behavior Intervention Plan before your student's IEP meeting, you can build in proactive strategies from the beginning. You should work closely with your student's IEP team to develop these strategies.

## Observation-Based Assessments

Observation is the best way to evaluate troublesome behaviors, and as we discussed in Chapter 1, your observations of a student are the most authentic data available. Whether you're working with your school's early intervention team (for a student without an IEP) or your student's IEP team (for a student with an identified disability), the team can use your observation-based assessments as a starting point for making decisions about your student's program.

### Elements of Behavior

How your student behaves rarely exists in a vacuum. The effect of these elements should be taken into account in your OBAs:

- Context (*e.g., What is happening in your student's world at that time?*)

- Environment (*e.g., How big is the room? How many children are present?*)

- Emotional state of your student (*e.g., Was there a recent family trauma or disagreement with another youngster?*)

- Physical state of your student (*e.g., Is he or she tired, hungry, or sick?*),

- Student expectations (*e.g., Your student expects you to ignore his or her behavior because it's ignored at home.*)

### Principles of Observation-Based Assessments

Keep the following principles in mind as you observe your student:

**Don't jump to conclusions.** Be careful to note only what you see your student do. Stay objective. Resist making assumptions about his or her intentions (e.g., trying to annoy, trying to get attention, boredom) until you have sufficient information. While problem behaviors serve a purpose for your student, "why" he or she does something may seem totally unrelated at first to "what" he or she does. For example, Frank might continually bother Catherine because he's jealous of the attention she gets from you, while Darryl's efforts to annoy Maria are attempts to let her know he likes her. Unsuccessful interventions are often due to premature or incorrect judgments about "why" a student acts a certain way.

**Be comprehensive.** To determine which behaviors you'll address, you should collect several observations of your student's behavior. Ask fellow team members to help you make observations in various settings or situations. Make observations in different environments, such as a special area class (e.g., physical education), or during transitions (e.g., moving from one class or activity to another), as well as during different kinds of classroom activities (e.g., a small group discussion, large group listening activity, or independent work time). Just like CBAs, OBAs are a comprehensive collection of data.

**Target behavior.** Determine which behavior is most troublesome (e.g., calling out in class, disrespectful comments, or physically hurting other students). Ask yourself: *If I could change one thing my student does, what would it be?* If you have difficulty targeting only one behavior, make observations of your student in several environments and look for the one or two inappropriate behaviors that happen most often.

**Focus on what you can do.** Several of the elements that affect behavior occur outside of school. Some of them can cause serious emotional or behavioral problems (e.g., students who live in abusive homes, youngsters who are exposed to drugs, crime, or gang violence, or those caught between quarreling divorced parents). School personnel typically have little control over such factors. Be mindful that despite valiant efforts by classroom teachers, administrators, and social service staff, attempts to improve your student's life outside of school may prove fruitless. Focus your work where you have more influence and can be most successful—in the classroom or school environment.

## Functional Behavioral Assessments

Whether your student has an IEP or not, the process you use to observe behavior is essentially the same. *A Functional Behavioral Assessment* (FBA) is a series of steps you follow to observe and understand your student's problem behavior. There are six main steps in an FBA:

**Clarify the behavior.** With your team, identify and agree upon the exact behavior that needs to change. Be as specific as possible. Global descriptions of behavioral expectations (e.g., treat other students nicely or behave appropriately in a group) will not be as helpful as specific behavioral expectations (e.g., refrain from physically hurting other students, or comply with teacher requests). The identified problem behavior should be concrete and measurable. (*Take a look at Tool 2.1 on page 29. It's a sample chart of specific positive and negative behaviors you can observe.*)

**Determine antecedents.** Through observations and interviews, collect information about where and when the problem behaviors occur and don't occur. A thorough review of your student's records will help uncover conditions outside of school that may contribute to troublesome behaviors (e.g., recent divorce, trauma in the home or neighborhood, change in your student's medications). Ask these questions: *What's different about the places where the misbehavior does and doesn't happen? Is the behavior likely to occur at a specific time of day or in a certain setting? Are there circumstances that consistently arise prior to the problem behavior (e.g., social conflicts, adult requests, task difficulty)?*

**Identify current consequences.** Using the information you've collected, carefully review what happens as a result of your student's behavior (e.g., he/she gains attention from the teacher or other students, avoids the task, or gets something he/she wants). The consequences of your student's behavior may be positive or negative, but even negative results can be reinforcing for some students, causing the problem behavior to occur again. For example, when Ron's teacher asks him to read a passage from the text, he refuses. Consequently, his teacher removes the text from Ron's desk and tells him to sit there and do nothing—exactly what Ron wanted in the first place.

**Collect baseline data.** As discussed in Chapter 1, gather your observations before you introduce any interventions. Carefully document the antecedents and consequences of your student's misbehavior. This will give you your *baseline data. (See Tool 2.2 on page 30: this Behavior Observation Form illustrates one way to make these observations.)* It shows baseline data collected on a student's behavior by an observer watching the interaction between the teacher and student. Typically, you'll need at least three days of baseline data. In a crisis situation, however, you might shorten how much initial data you collect before you intervene. For example, if your student is physically hurting other students, you wouldn't allow him or her to do it for three days without intervening.

**Develop a hypothesis.** With your team, develop a hypothesis about why the problem behavior occurs. This statement is your "best guess" regarding the function of your student's troublesome behavior. Two common functions of misbehavior are: 1) to "gain" something (e.g., attention, approval, or desired materials), or 2) to "avoid" something (e.g., a difficult task, an unwanted activity, or interaction with certain individuals). To predict where and when a behavior will likely occur, decide what you think the function of the behavior is. For instance, if Jackie has temper tantrums before leaving the room for a special class each day, one reason might be that she doesn't like going to that class. Another reason might be that transitions out of your classroom are difficult for her. If so, Jackie might act out whenever it's time to move to another location.

**Test your hypothesis.** Change one of the variables (e.g., setting, time of day, antecedent, consequence) of your hypothesis to see if the problem behavior still occurs. For instance, if you conclude that Juan makes inappropriate verbal outbursts whenever he sits near a particular peer group because he gains their attention and laughter, move him away from that group. *Does his problem behavior get worse or better?*

# Observable Positive and Negative Behaviors Chart

## Attention and Organization Skills

| Negative Behaviors | Positive Behaviors |
|---|---|
| Moves about or leaves classroom | Stays in assigned area |
| Doesn't follow verbal directions | Responds to verbal directions |
| Forgets or has difficulty transferring information | Uses learned information in a different setting |
| Doesn't pay attention | Visually attends to speaker |
| Perseverates or has difficulty with transitions | Moves smoothly from one activity to the next |
| Is distracted by sounds or people in the immediate area | Maintains attention to task |
| Loses possessions or has a messy work area | Shows responsibility for personal property |

## Group and Social Relationship Skills

| Negative Behaviors | Positive Behaviors |
|---|---|
| Acts out when others receive praise or attention | Follows classroom rules to gain praise or recognition |
| Is physically aggressive with adults or peers | Refrains from physically hurting others |
| Calls out in group or class discussions | Raises hand and responds when called on |
| Makes noises or inappropriate comments | Listens and responds appropriately |
| Makes profane comments to teachers | Speaks in a respectful manner |
| Doesn't share materials or space with others | Works cooperatively with other students |
| Destroys or steals others' possessions | Asks permission to touch others' possessions |
| Touches others inappropriately | Keeps hands away from others |

## Mood and Motivation

| Negative Behaviors | Positive Behaviors |
|---|---|
| Refuses to follow directions | Complies with teacher requests |
| Is tardy or absent from school or class without an acceptable excuse | Regularly attends class on time |
| Becomes easily upset by constructive criticism | Responds positively to teacher suggestions |
| Whines, cries, or has temper tantrums | Remains positively engaged in activity |
| Hurts himself or destroys his possessions | Improves his appearance or expresses positive feelings about himself |
| Hands in incomplete assignments or messy work with careless errors | Completes assignments accurately within designated time period |
| Copies or seeks inordinate amounts of assistance to complete work | Completes assignments independently |

**Tool 2.2**

# Behavior Observation Form

**Student:** Jackie S.

**Observation Date:** _____

**Observer:** Ms. Allen

**Time:** 10:30–10:45

**Class Activity:** Art Project

| ANTECEDENT | BEHAVIOR | CONSEQUENCE |
|---|---|---|
| What happens before the behavior | What specific action student takes | What happens after the behavior |
| Teacher asks students to look at her. | Jackie looks at a pencil sitting on Charlie's desk (next to her desk). | Teacher says "Pay attention, Jackie." |
| Teacher gives directions for art project. | Jackie watches teacher. | No feedback or verbal praise to Jackie. |
| Charlie begins rolling his pencil back and forth on his desk. | Jackie grabs Charlie's pencil. | Charlie yells. |
| Teacher tells Jackie to give the pencil back. | Jackie refuses. | No feedback to Jackie. Teacher is distracted by a student asking a question and turns toward the other student. |
| Charlie tries to grab pencil from Jackie and hits her in the arm. | Jackie punches Charlie in the face. | Charlie cries. Teacher comes over, takes pencil from Jackie, gives it back to Charlie, and sends Jackie to the office. |

## Developing a Behavior Intervention Plan

After you form and test your hypothesis about your student's problem behavior, you're ready to develop a Behavior Intervention Plan (BIP). Your student's BIP defines what new behaviors you'll teach, how you'll teach these behaviors, and how you'll reinforce your student's success. Use the data you gathered during the Functional Behavioral Assessment as a guide for writing your student's BIP. (See Tool 2.3, a

sample Behavior Intervention Plan, on page 32.) To develop an effective BIP, consider the following procedures:

**Determine substitute behaviors.** Once you know the function of your student's misbehavior, you can identify more positive, behaviors that can serve the same function. Choose a desired behavior you'll teach your student to use instead of the problem behavior. *Does it serve the same function? Is it* *observable and measurable? Is it a typical behavior for other students?*

**Identify environmental or setting changes.**
You should also look at how to neutralize or eliminate the situations that trigger the troublesome behavior (antecedents). Sometimes, by changing some aspects of the environment, you can prevent the problem behavior from occuring. For example, if you determine a student is consistently tardy to class because he or she is hungry and stops to eat a snack on the way to the classroom, you can solve the problem by allowing the student to eat a small snack in the room at the beginning of class.

**Describe necessary prompts or conditions.**
Consider what specific conditions will signal or encourage your student to use the new "desired behavior" instead of the problem behavior. These conditions might include visual cues or teacher prompts. For instance, if you want Thomas to stop calling out answers during a group discussion, you might display a stop sign when you want him to listen and a picture of a hand when you want him to raise his hand. For an older student, you might develop a secret signal, such as touching your ear, when you want him to raise his hand.

**Define strategies.** Your student needs to learn a new behavior. You and your team should select which specific strategies will be most successful for teaching this new skill. *Will you use role play? Will you use teacher or peer modeling? How will you explain the new expectations to your student?*

**Prepare for when things go wrong.** Even great plans can go wrong. You and your team should

consider what variables could impede your student's success. For example, if your student has a conflict with a peer on the bus, he or she could start the day upset. Your student may need time and a place to "cool down" before going to class. Look back at the FBA to help you predict and prepare for circumstances that could interfere. *What can be done to prevent a crisis or problematic situation? What should you do if the problem behavior reappears?*

**Specify reinforcement.** Define specific rewards or reinforcers that will encourage your student to continue to use the new behavior. Remember that different things work with different students. If appropriate, ask your student what type of positive consequence he or she would prefer. Typical reinforcers include praise or stickers but there are many more. *(The Ways To Encourage Positive Behaviors sidebar, on page 33, includes a variety of reinforcers your student can earn.)*

**Collect data to evaluate the plan.** Decide how you'll measure the success of your BIP. Select a practical, simple way to collect data on your student's behavior. Your data will tell you if the plan is working. *(See Tool 2.4 on page 34: the Behavior Observation Tally Sheet demonstrates how Juan's teacher tallied his calling-out behavior.)* Decide how often you'll collect data on your student's behavior—several times a day, daily, or weekly. What type of data will you collect—frequency count, duration measure, interval checks? How will you visually represent your data—line graph, bar graph? *(Tool 2.5, Possible Data Collection Methods, on page 35, shows various types of data collection you can use with different behaviors.)*

**Tool 2.3**

# Behavior Intervention Plan

**Student:** _Jackie S._        **Grade:** _1st_

**Date:** _____    **Teacher:** _Mr. Kelly_

## Results of Functional Behavioral Assessment

| ANTECEDENTS | SPECIFIC BEHAVIOR | CONSEQUENCES | FUNCTION |
|---|---|---|---|
| Teacher gives verbal directions. | Jackie looks at objects in room.<br><br>Jackie doesn't follow directions. | Teacher says "Pay attention." | ☒ Gains peer attention<br>☒ Gains teacher attention<br>☐ Gains approval<br>☒ Gains item/material |
| Peer displays or plays with personal item. | Jackie takes item that belongs to peer.<br><br>Jackie refuses to comply with teacher request. | Peer yells, cries, or takes items back.<br><br>Sent to office. | ☐ Avoids task<br>☐ Avoids stimulation<br>☐ Avoids individual(s)<br>☐ Other<br>_____ |

Frequency of occurrence: _10_ (number) incidents per ____ hour, _x_ day, ____ week, ____ month

Duration of occurrence: From ____ (circle time) minutes or hours   to ____ minutes or hours

**Interventions used to date:**

   _Teacher ignores_____    Effective ____    Ineffective _x_

   _Teacher reprimands_____    Effective ____    Ineffective _x_

   _Teacher redirects_____    Effective _x_    Ineffective ____

## Intervention Plan

**Desired Behavior:** _Jackie will maintain attention to task for 10-minute intervals._

| INTERVENTION(S) | LOCATION | REINFORCER(S) | PERSON(S) RESPONSIBLE |
|---|---|---|---|
| Verbal redirection<br><br>Silent signal from teacher<br><br>Teacher proximity during verbal directions to class | Classroom | Verbal praise and points earned per 10-minute interval for extra time on computer | Mr. Kelly |

**Process to Monitor Intervention:** How Often: ____ Daily _x_ Weekly ____ Monthly

Monitoring Method: _x_ Formal Observation ____ Student Conference ____ Parent Conference

**Evidence of Accomplishment:** _____ for 30 minutes (three 10-minute intervals) in 4 out of 5 days

Students respond to a variety of reinforcers and rewards. Consider these for your Behavior Intervention Plan:

### Tangible Rewards—Something Your Students Can Get

Award certificates
Award ribbons
Candy or snack food, such as pretzels or veggie sticks
Collectible item, such as a colorful rock or picture
Coupons for free ice cream or snack in the cafeteria
Coupons for one night free from homework
Note of praise sent home to parents
Pencil, gel pen, pencil top, or eraser
Prize from a special "super star" prize box
Smiley face on paper
Small stickers or stars on a sticker chart
Large stickers on hand or shirt

### Activity Reinforcers—Something Your Students Can Do:

**Extra time to:**
Play at recess
Draw on the chalkboard
Draw pictures on special paper
Play a board game
Read a favorite book
Play in the gym

**Opportunities to:**
Be the teacher
Run errands
Read aloud to the class
Bring parents or an invited guest to school
Be teacher's helper, principal's helper, or office or library helper
Help out in or read in another classroom
Be first in line
Take a book from your book collection home for the week
Take a special stuffed animal home for the night
Take a trip to a museum, scenic spot, or nature center
Have a lunchbox party in your classroom
Have a popcorn, ice cream, or pizza party
Have lunch with you or the principal

**Time to use:**
Computer
Rubber stamp
Special markers
Shaving cream to paint the top of the desk

# Behavior Observation Tally Sheet

**Student:** Juan G.                  **Observer:** Mr. Keeley

**Target Behavior:** Inappropriate verbal comments

**Date of Observation:** _____     **Setting & Activity:** Class discussion

**Type of Measurement:** __x__ Frequency     _____ Duration     _____ Interval

| START TIME | STOP TIME | TALLY OR INTERVALS | | | | | | | | | | TOTAL |
|---|---|---|---|---|---|---|---|---|---|---|---|---|
| | | 1 | 2 | 3 | 4 | 5 | 6 | 7 | 8 | 9 | 10 | |
| 9:00 | 9:10 | ✓ | ✓ | ✓ | ✓ | | | | | | | 4 |
| 9:10 | 9:20 | ✓ | ✓ | | | | | | | | | 2 |
| 9:20 | 9:30 | ✓ | ✓ | ✓ | | | | | | | | 3 |
| | | | | | | | | | | | | |
| | | | | | | | | | | | | |
| | | | | | | | | | | | | |
| | | | | | | | | | | | | |

**Behavior count:** 9 in 30 minutes   **Average duration:** _____   **Percentage:** _____

**Additional observations or comments:** Juan's comments were directed at his peers. They were funny and seemed to be attempts to gain their attention. He offered only one "on-task" verbal comment between 9:10 and 9:20. Ninety percent of Juan's comments were inappropriate.

**Discuss maintenance and generalization.**
Remember to share your student's BIP with all staff members who will be responsible for his or her program. You and your team should determine how your student will show he or she has learned the desired behavior. Usually, a new behavior must be used consistently for at least five to seven weeks before you move on. *How long does your student need to use the new behavior before you fade the reinforcements or supports? How will you encourage your student to generalize the new behavior to new situations or settings?*

# Possible Data Collection Methods

| **BEHAVIORS** | **TYPE OF DATA COLLECTION** |
|---|---|
| **Behaviors that last for a period of time, for example:** | **Duration** |
| ☑ being out of seat for a time period | **What to record:** Note when the behavior begins and when it ends. |
| ☑ crying | **What to use:** Stop watch, clock, video tape, egg timer |
| ☑ daydreaming | |
| ☑ perseverating on a behavior | |
| ☑ playing with items in desk | |
| ☑ attending to speaker | |
| **Behaviors that occur as separate or recurring events, for example:** | **Frequency** |
| ☑ getting in and out of seat | **What to record:** Record each time the behavior occurs as a tally during a set time period. |
| ☑ hitting or touching others | **What to use:** Pennies or tokens moved from pocket to pocket; chips or tokens put in a container; stickers, happy faces, or stars put on charts. |
| ☑ losing or taking others' possessions | |
| ☑ making noises | |
| ☑ raising hand | |
| ☑ asking to leave the room | |
| ☑ talking back to teacher | |
| ☑ being tardy for class | |
| ☑ using profanity | |
| ☑ yelling out in class or verbal outbursts | |
| ☑ temper tantrums | |
| ☑ completing work | |
| **Behaviors that are inconsistently or not easily observed, for example:** | **Interval** |
| ☑ attending to task or attending to distractions | **What to record:** Select a length of time (e.g., one minute). Observe the student at each interval and note "+" if the behavior is present or "–" if the behavior is not present. |
| ☑ refusing to follow directions | **What to use:** Marks on masking tape on wrist; checks on post-it notes, mailing labels, or index cards. |
| ☑ talking in class | |
| ☑ whining | |
| ☑ moving smoothly between activities | |

# Classroom and School Strategies

Even the best Behavior Intervention Plan can be ineffective in an atmosphere of general disorder. Your students will learn best in a structured classroom where there are clear expectations. Likewise, your school atmosphere should encourage positive behavior. IDEA recognized the importance of fostering an effective learning environment for all students, suggesting that teachers and schools take a proactive approach to challenging behaviors.

## Classroom Behavioral Supports

Effective teachers use proactive strategies in their classrooms to prevent behavior problems. When your classroom behavioral support skills are successful, your students are working in a constructive manner and are actively involved in learning. Occasionally, students misbehave even in the best-run classrooms. To stop your student's misbehavior from growing into chronic classroom disruption or disorder, you should reflect on how effective your classroom techniques are. Here are a few selected ideas about classroom behavioral supports:

**Physical arrangement.** Organizing the space in your classroom can create a positive learning atmosphere. Divide the classroom into defined spaces for specific purposes. Clarify procedures for moving through "high traffic" areas, such as the entranceway to the classroom. Orderly classroom displays limit distractions. Removing unused equipment and covering storage areas will decrease unnecessary stimulation in the room. Be mindful of the noise level near certain items, such as a fish tank or pencil sharpener. If you can, set aside a "quiet place" for students to work or calm down by using study carrels, freestanding bookcases, or bulletin boards.

**Set clear rules and expectations.** Describe your classroom rules in positive behavioral statements and post them in the room where they are visible to all students. A concrete rule, such as "Raise your hand and wait your turn to speak" is more positive than "Don't shout out" and more specific than "Be polite."

**Define expected consequences.** Consequences for breaking the rules should be fair and enforced consistently. Initially, you may need to state the penalties for misbehavior several times to be sure your students understand them. If your students break a rule, ask them to explain the consequence of their actions.

**Correct minor rule violations in a matter-of-fact way.** Don't waste time on minor infractions. When students break a minor rule, remind them what the expected behavior is and then move on. Refocus your students on the learning activity as quickly as you can.

**Establish routines.** Develop set procedures for how you want things done in your classroom. *Where and when do students submit work assignments? How will you alert students that an activity is about to end? How do you want students to enter or leave the classroom?*

**Reward generously.** Be quick to compliment and reinforce those students who follow the rules. Saying "Thank you for sitting down quietly" to one student can be an incentive to others to do the same thing. Build in reward systems that all students can earn for following the rules, such as a party at the end of the term or extra recess time at week's end.

If you're interested in exploring the topic of classroom behavioral support techniques in depth, there are many excellent resources available. Several are listed in the Resource section.

### School-Wide Behavioral Policies

All students need to learn how to work together and support one another as a community of learners. When your school implements positive behavioral strategies, all students benefit. Currently, many experts advocate an emphasis on teaching positive behaviors. However, some of the more typical school-wide approaches focus on penalties. Here are several examples:

**School discipline policy.** Your school's discipline policy or code of conduct outlines general behavior expectations, types of infractions, and the consequences for violations. All students, including students with disabilities, should be aware of the discipline policy and expected to abide by it. In general, a student with disabilities can be disciplined in the same way as other students as long as it doesn't result in a change of placement (more about this later). If your student violates the discipline policy, you should work with your administrators to enforce the appropriate punishment in a fair and consistent manner.

**Zero-tolerance policy.** Many school districts have adopted zero-tolerance policies to address serious behaviors, such as physically harming someone or bringing a weapon or drugs to school. As the name implies, these policies have defined, absolute punishments

for violations that often result in suspensions or expulsions from school. Zero-tolerance policies have been criticized because they often don't take into account the student's age or understanding of the rules. To be effective, your school's policy should clearly state which behaviors will lead to removal from school, and all students and their parents should be aware of them.

**Suspensions and expulsions.** For serious discipline code or zero-tolerance policy violations, such as fighting, the consequence often is suspension, or even expulsion, from school. If your student doesn't have an IEP, he or she may be suspended or expelled. If your student has an IEP, he or she can be removed from school but certain factors apply. *(See the Disciplining Students with Disabilities sidebar on page 38 for more information.)*

## Positive School-Wide and District-Wide Programs

Keep in mind that your school's discipline and zero-tolerance policies are essentially punishment plans. For some students, the threat of punishment is enough to encourage good behavior. For many students with challenging behaviors, however, it's not.

Today's school leaders now realize we need to approach discipline problems in a more positive way. To build a school climate that's safe and conducive to learning, we must teach appropriate behavior. As discussed previously, you can begin that process in your own classroom by using sound classroom behavioral support techniques.

# DISCIPLINING STUDENTS WITH DISABILITIES

IDEA '97 regulations offered the following options to school personnel when disciplining students with disabilities:

**Removals for up to ten school days at a time**—A student with a disability can be removed for up to ten consecutive school days.

**Additional removals of up to ten school days**—A student may be removed for separate acts of misconduct as long as the removals don't form a pattern or appear to be a change in the student's educational placement.

**Access to instruction or services**—Schools don't need to provide a student with access to instruction or services for the first ten days unless they do it for students who are not disabled. For removals that extend beyond the first ten days, schools must provide instruction and services to allow a student to make appropriate progress toward his or her IEP goals. The administrator and the student's special education teacher will decide how to do this. Usually, some homebound instruction or placement in an interim alternative educational setting is considered.

**Removals for more than ten school days**—If a student has violated a school rule that requires him or her to be removed for more than ten school days at a time, or if the student has previously been removed from school as a discipline procedure for at least 10 school days, the IEP team must meet to consider whether the misconduct was a manifestation of the student's disability. To decide this, the team must complete a Functional Behavioral Assessment. If a student's IEP team decides that the student's misconduct is not related to, or the result of, a disability, the student may be removed from school. However, the school still needs to provide services. If the IEP team decides the behavior is a manifestation of the student's disability, the student may not be removed from school. To be proactive, we strongly recommend that the IEP team develop a Behavior Intervention Plan to address problem behaviors of those students who will likely misbehave. If typical consequences for a student's misbehavior can't be applied, the BIP will give you guidance about alternative consequences.

**Removals for weapons, drugs, or dangerous behavior**—If a student brings a dangerous weapon or drugs to school, or is likely to harm him or herself or others, the student can be removed from school for up to 45 days to an *interim alternative educational setting*.

In addition, your school should adopt a school-wide program that teaches all students self-control and social skills strategies. If your school doesn't yet have one, you may want to advocate for one. School-wide or district-wide positive behavioral support programs usually include these elements:

- A school or district committee that examines discipline policies and helps develop new strategies.

- A set of clearly stated positive expectations for behavior (*e.g., school rules, character principles*).

- Procedures for teaching desired behaviors (*e.g., a specific curriculum, role-playing activities, modeling procedures*).

- A system of continuous reinforcement or rewards to encourage students to practice correct behaviors (*e.g., good character or good citizenship awards, sticker incentive programs*).

- A support system for students with serious emotional or behavioral problems (*e.g., behavior management team, crisis team, links to community mental health services*).

- Alternative educational settings for those students who need them.

There are many types of school-wide and district-wide programs that address improving school climate and student behavior. If you're interested in more information on these types of approaches, several are listed in the Resources section.

## KEY POINTS

You can provide a positive learning environment for all your students by:

1. Identifying problem behaviors early through Observation-Based Assessments.

2. Assisting your student's team to conduct a Functional Behavioral Assessment.

3. Helping your student's team develop and implement a Behavior Intervention Plan.

4. Using positive, consistent classroom management strategies in your classroom.

5. Working with your administrators to enforce the school and district discipline policies.

6. Advocating for school-wide and district-wide positive behavioral supports for all students.

# 3 The Collaborative Team Process

*"Alone, we can do so little. Together, we can do so much."*

Helen Keller

It used to be very easy to feel "alone" in a school. Most of us prepared to teach under an isolated practice model: a single teacher working in a single classroom, teaching a single subject area or grade level. Each teacher had responsibility for his or her curriculum and students. It could be lonely, but comfortable.

Schools have changed. Figuratively, the classroom doors are open as students, support staff, teachers, parents, and even community members move dynamically from one learning event to another. In today's schools, we're all expected to work together to meet common goals. We're encouraged to share responsibility for curriculum and students, including students with disabilities.

As a result, you may find yourself in a classroom working side-by-side with a special education teacher, general education teacher, or paraeducator. Often general education teachers and special educators jointly instruct small groups or even an entire class of students.

Today, teamwork is crucial. It's the cornerstone for ensuring that students with needs receive quality instruction. You need to know how to function in a team, whether or not your student has an IEP. If your student does have an IEP, teamwork will help you assess your student's needs, develop IEP expectations, and implement the IEP.

This chapter will explore various ways that you and other staff members can work together using a collaborative team process to help your students suceed.

## Chapter 3 Toolkit

**Tool 3.1**
Team Teaching/Co-Teaching Daily Lesson Plan

**Tool 3.2**
Sequence-of-the-Day Planning Sheet

**Tool 3.3**
Special Area Class Communication Form (**in Appendix**)

# How Teams Work

Education today is a collaborative process. It's a wonder then, why so few school team members have any preparation for participating on a collaborative team. A common expectation for all educators is cooperating with other team members. How you interact with the instructional team in your school directly affects your student's progress.

## Types of Teams

As a team member, your responsibilities depend on what kind of team you're working with. Let's look at some team models:

**Multidisciplinary**. As its name implies, team members on a multidisciplinary team represent different disciplines or job positions. If you're on a multidisciplinary team, you'll present your own perspective about your student separately, with little consideration for other areas. A high school interdepartmental team and a typical IEP team are examples of multidisciplinary teams.

**Interdisciplinary.** An interdisciplinary team does more sharing than a multidisciplinary team. As a member of an interdisciplinary team, you'll still present your own perspective about your student, but there is some effort to discuss how your opinion intersects with those of other team members. Your information may be included in one report that you write jointly with other team members. You may also share instructional responsibilities with other members. Often, early childhood intervention teams and middle school instructional teams are interdisciplinary teams.

**Transdisciplinary.** The whole purpose of a transdisciplinary team is to function as one ("across disciplines"). If you are part of a transdisciplinary team, your opinions will be blended with others into one fully shared statement. You'll have joint responsibility for all the goals in a transdisciplinary IEP. Some examples of transdisciplinary teaming are transition service teams, birth-to-three family service teams, and teams that service students with severe disabilities.

## Characteristics of Collaborative Teams

No matter what type of team your school has, you should become familiar with the collaborative team process. If your team is using collaborative decision-making, you'll see these characteristics:

**Shared purpose.** All team members share the same "vision" or "mission." There is a sense of purpose among team members.

**Cohesiveness.** A relaxed "atmosphere" exists with no obvious tensions. Team members treat each other with respect and feel a sense of "togetherness" within the group.

**Competence.** Each team member is competent at her job or in his discipline area.

**Focus.** Discussion is focused on the task at hand. If it goes off topic, someone brings the group back to the point.

**Open discussion.** Everyone listens and feels comfortable offering an opinion and encouraging others to share their thoughts.

Thoughtful questions are raised as important points to consider.

**Open disagreement.** Team members value other opinions, understanding that differences of opinion are unavoidable and that differing thoughts lead to creative solutions. When team members disagree, they do so frankly without personal attacks. Interpersonal disagreements are quickly resolved.

**Consensus.** Most decisions are reached by "consensus," meaning general agreement with no strong feelings of opposition within the group.

**Shared responsibilities.** Tasks are assigned and responsibilities accepted and shared, as needed.

**Good leadership.** The team leader doesn't dominate or demand that others defer to him or her. Leadership of the group could change from time to time as the subject or situation warrants.

**Ongoing reflection.** The team is reflective about its work, occasionally reviewing its own operations.

**Synergy.** There is a sense of "synergy" among the team—that what they do together has a combined impact greater than the sum of each individual's efforts.

# Collaborative Instruction

Regardless of what role you play on the team (e.g., general education teacher, special education teacher, related service provider, or paraeducator), you must cooperate with others in your school to implement a student's instructional plan.

## Models of Collaborative Instruction

Following is an explanation of the main kinds of collaborative teaching models. Most likely, some versions of these are present in your school. *Note:* special education "staff" in the following descriptions refers to special education teachers, related service providers (e.g., speech-language pathologists, occupational therapists, etc.), paraeducators, or other instructional staff members (e.g., adapted physical education teachers, music therapists, etc.).

**Team teaching.** One or more general education teachers join with a special education staff member to form a teaching team. Everyone shares responsibility as an equal partner for planning, instructing, assessing, and grading all the students in the classroom. Most often, you'll see team teaching in a preschool or elementary school, but it can be done in any school.

**Co-teaching.** The general education teacher and special education staff member teach alongside each other in the same classroom. They may co-teach for one period or for several classes during the week. The general education teacher usually maintains grading responsibilities but shares planning, instructing, and assessing tasks. You'll find co-teaching in many schools, especially middle and high schools. *(See Tool 3.1 on page 44: the Team Teaching/ Co-Teaching Daily Lesson Plan shows one way to develop shared lesson plans for team teachers.)*

# Team Teaching/Co-Teaching Daily Lesson Plan

This shared lesson plan helps the general education teacher and the special education teacher communicate and plan with one another. It also helps the team document what types of accommodations are needed in the general education classroom.

**Class/Subject:**  Grade 4/Social Studies

**General Classroom Teacher:**  Mr. Holmes       **Special Education Staff:**  Mrs. Sutton

| Date | What are you going to teach (content)? | How will the class be grouped? | What are the key points of the lesson? | What materials are needed? | Which students need accommodations? | How will you evaluate learning (product)? |
|---|---|---|---|---|---|---|
| 11/15 | Native American dwellings | Cooperative learning groups | Dwelling names | Worksheet, p. 5 | Peer partner–Hillary Graphic organizer–Tom | Worksheet completion 90% accuracy |
|  |  |  | 4 tribes | Worksheet, p. 5 | Peer partner–Hillary Graphic organizer–Tom |  |
|  |  | Class discussion | Climate | Text | Highlighted text–Ann Key vocabulary list–Ann | Oral responses, 80% in 4 out of 5 attempts |
|  |  |  | Function of homes | Text | Highlighted text–Ann Key vocabulary list–Ann |  |

**Parallel teaching.** Also called "push-in" services, the special education staff member works with a small group of students in a section of the general education classroom. Both students with disabilities and at-risk students may be included in the group. Ideally, the special education staff member works on content and skills linked with the general education curriculum. Each team member takes responsibility for his or her own planning, instructing, and assessing. This model is mostly seen in elementary schools.

**Supported instruction.** This is typically called "pull-out" services. To be truly collaborative, the general education teacher and the special education staff member must plan together. Both focus their instruction on similar topics or themes. The general education teacher covers the concepts and vocabulary while the special education staff member provides pre-teaching, directed practice, hands-on exercises, and structured review of the core curriculum concepts. Each team member takes responsibility for his or her own planning and instructing, but the general education teacher continues to be responsible for assessing and grading the students. This model can be effective in any school.

**Continuum of instructional options.** A continuum of instructional options should be available to meet the individualized needs of all students, especially those with disabilities. Several hybrids of the above models also exist in some schools. Instructional specialists, such as reading teachers and special education teachers, co-teach in a few general education classrooms for part of the day and provide supported instruction as a "pull-out" for the other part of the day. However, the logistics of working in multiple roles in several general education classrooms can be very difficult, even overwhelming, for these teachers.

### Working as an Instructional Team

Whether you're a general education teacher or a special education staff member, you bring expertise and special skills to the Instructional Team. General education teachers are content specialists, while special education teachers and specialists are well versed in instructional strategies and modifications. To effectively meet your students' needs, your instructional team should have the following attributes:

**Shared goals.** Your student's intervention plan or IEP should be available to all team members who are responsible for his or her instructional program. Everyone on the team needs to be aware of the IEP goals and objectives. Sharing responsibility for goals helps give the team a joint focus.

**Clear expectations.** Team members should openly discuss their responsibilities and their expectations of other team members. It's helpful to list roles and responsibilities. *(See the Roles and Responsibilities for Team Teaching sidebar on page 46.)*

**Effective communication.** Frequent opportunities for contact help the team avoid misunderstandings. Your team should determine how often to meet. You should also consider what formal and informal communication avenues you'll use (e.g., E-mail, phone conference, joint planning forms, shared lesson plans, shared student study guides).

**Role release.** After working together for a period of time, many team members report they feel comfortable enough with each other's skills to exchange activities or tasks with one another. For example, a general education teacher might ask a specialist to teach a lesson to the entire class while she works individually with a struggling student. Or, a speech-language pathologist might want a paraeducator to practice a speech skill with one student while he works on a language lesson with a small group.

## The Forgotten Team Members

Your Instructional Team probably includes at least one general education classroom teacher and one or more special education staff members. But there are other members of the team who tend to be overlooked.

# ROLES AND RESPONSIBILITIES FOR TEAM TEACHING

## A. Responsibilities of the General Education Teacher

1. Determine concepts necessary to meet curriculum objectives.

2. Identify goals and objectives of the course.

3. Teach specific class content.

4. Provide knowledge on scope and sequence of content area.

5. Determine key points of a lesson.

6. Utilize various instructional strategies to deliver and evaluate instruction.

## B. Responsibilities of the Special Education Teacher

1. Teach study skills and learning strategies.

2. Develop study guides.

3. Collect data on student performance.

4. Provide diagnostic information on academic levels and learning styles of special education students.

5. Adapt textbooks, assignments, and tests.

## C. Shared Responsibilities

1. Plan instructional activities to achieve goals/objectives of course or grade level.

2. Select and order classroom materials and supplemental aids.

3. Establish grading procedures.

4. Establish classroom management plan.

5. Give individual assistance to students.

6. Instruct entire class.

7. Maintain home contact.

8. Develop effective teaching practices.

9. Share effective teaching practices with other educators.

Developed by Joyce Emmett, Danbury Public Schools, Danbury, CT.

## Special Area Teachers

All the students in your school probably participate in art, music, media or library, and physical education classes, but those teachers are rarely included in collaborative planning. Building a collaborative relationship with special area teachers is important and can present unique issues when you are working with students who have special needs:

**Generalized instruction.** Most special area teachers were never required or taught how to individualize instruction. Therefore, students with disabilities in their classrooms may be expected to do what all the other students in the class are doing, regardless of what's written in their IEPs. You should make an effort to see that the special area teachers in your school are aware of your student's intervention plan or IEP goals and objectives.

**Minimal accommodations.** Special area teachers often lack knowledge about how to use accommodations or modifications in their classes. In addition, they're rarely asked to provide information for an IEP. As a result, intervention plans and IEPs may not address the special area's learning environment. Before your student's plan is developed, ask your special area teachers for their input. Afterwards, you should discuss the accommodations your student needs with the special area teachers.

**Class size.** Some schools double, triple, and even quadruple general education classes into one large, noisy, even chaotic special area class. Class management is a major concern. Including a student with a disability in such an environment can be frustrating and nonproductive. Check to see if there are smaller classes, such as adaptive physical education classes or music therapy sessions, that might be more appropriate for your student to attend. Perhaps you can arrange for your student to attend part of the special area class and spend the rest of the period in one-to-one instruction with a paraeducator or specialist on related skills (e.g., after attending part of a physical education class, your student could work with a paraeducator on

dressing skills in the locker room, or after participating in part of an art class, your student could work on eye-hand coordination skills with the occupational therapist). These should be considerations in drawing up your student's plan.

**Lack of knowledge.** Most special area teachers receive very little preparation for teaching students with disabilities. They may have limited hands-on experience as well. Offer to provide your special area teachers with background information on your student's disability and ways to teach him or her. If you can, include special area teachers in professional development opportunities that will help them learn how to work with students with disabilities.

**Limited personnel support.** In order to include students with disabilities in special area classes, IEP teams often assign a paraeducator to accompany them. Many paraeducators are unaware of the type of supports needed in special area classes. To complicate matters further, the paraeducator may hover around the student so much that he or she is socially isolated from other students in the class. Make sure the paraeducator clearly understands how to support the student in a special area class environment. You may want to observe the class to provide consultation for both the special area teacher and the paraeducator. Sometimes other students in the class can serve as effective peer tutors, if properly trained and supervised. *(The Special Area Class Communication Form, included in the Appendix, will help you communicate more effectively with special area teachers in your school.)*

### Paraeducators

All students have contact with education support staff, such as bus drivers, cafeteria workers, and custodians. Depending on your students' needs, some of these individuals may be involved in supporting their instructional program. In particular, paraeducators play a major role in the education of many students with disabilities. Paraeducators are known by many different titles, including classroom assistant, educational assistant, paraprofessional, instructional aide, teacher assistant, teacher aide, and tutor. Paraeducators should be an integral part of your Collaborative Instructional Team. Actively including them on your team may involve these considerations:

**Assistance vs. independence.** Paraeducators are supposed to "assist" in providing services to students with disabilities. Too often, paraeducators are planning, instructing, and assessing students without appropriate supervision and guidance. Teachers should develop lesson plans while the paraeducator assists in implementing them. Check with paraeducators assigned to your students about their duties. Make sure they understand their assignments and their role in the students' instructional programs.

**Monitoring vs. supervising.** As the teacher, you'll monitor how well your student's program is implemented. You should not be responsible for hiring, firing, or supervising paraeducators in your building. That's the duty of the administration. Clarify who has supervisory responsibilities for the paraeducator assigned to your student.

**Supporting instruction.** Paraeducators may be involved in students' programs in a variety of ways. They may help students with personal needs (e.g., toileting, eating, etc.), or work with students individually on specific skill practice. Paraeducators may also work with small groups of students or monitor a student's behavior in a group. All of these roles require that the paraeducator be familiar with a student's plan. Share the pertinent instructional goals and objectives or benchmarks in your student's intervention plan or IEP with the paraeducator. Include the paraeducator in problem-solving and team decisions.

**Documentation.** In order to show progress, you must keep track of your student's performance. The paraeducator can help take data on your student's academic performance or behavior. This can free you to work with other students or on different skills. Make sure the paraeducator assigned to your student knows how to observe behavior and how to objectively collect data.

**Preparing materials.** Your student's IEP may say that materials have to be specially designed to accommodate his or her special learning needs. Paraeducators can assist you by preparing these materials. Be careful, however, not to abuse the help that paraeducators give you. Limit the clerical activities that you assign.

## Teaming for Students with Severe Needs

A growing number of general education classrooms now include students with severe disabilities for part or all of the school day.

These students may have cognitive delays (i.e., mental retardation), special health care needs (e.g., gastrostomies that require feeding through a stomach tube) or more than one disability (e.g., deaf-blind). Planning for students with severe needs presents your Collaborative Instructional Team with unique opportunities and challenges.

## Components of Inclusion

Some of the following ideas about inclusion may help you plan with your team:

**Accessibility.** Students with severe disabilities ought to attend the school they would attend if they weren't disabled. This belief suggests that all public schools must be physically accessible. Students should be in a general education classroom—a classroom with appropriate staffing, space, equipment, technology, programs and services—with children their own age.

**Normalization.** Students with disabilities need to have the same experiences and opportunities available to them as students who are not disabled. This means that if your class is visiting an aquarium as part of a unit on marine life, your students with severe disabilities should go also.

**Interdependence.** In addition to encouraging all students to become more independent, we know that interdependency is also an important life skill. We all rely on others in some way. While expanding independence skills, students with severe disabilities must develop communication and cooperation skills—the building blocks for forming relationships with others.

**Diversity.** If you only spend time with people who are just like you, who talk like you, and have the same interests and abilities as you do, you could begin to think that everyone is alike. This kind of isolation breeds bias and bigotry. Growing up surrounded by diversity, on the other hand, teaches us to appreciate each other's differences. Your students who aren't disabled will learn to respect those who are by interacting with them in your classroom.

**Natural proportions.** Grouping many students with disabilities into one classroom or school can be overwhelming. The principle of natural proportions says that your class should have the same percentage of students with disabilities as there are in the general population (approximately 10–12 percent). Approximately 2–3 percent of the general population have severe disabilities. So, a school of 300 students could have about 30 to 36 students with disabilities of any kind, and possibly six to nine of them would have severe disabilities. At the classroom level, your general education class of 25 students might include three students with disabilities of any kind and perhaps one might have severe disabilities.

**Partial participation.** Simply put, if students have severe disabilities that interfere with their ability to participate in classroom activities to the same extent as other students, they can still benefit by doing part of the activities. For example, if your class is making maps of the school, a student with severe disabilities may name items found in a school.

## Accessing the General Education Curriculum

Historically, many schools offered a dual curriculum—one for students in general education classrooms and one for students with disabilities, especially students with severe disabilities. IDEA required that students with disabilities have access to the general education curriculum. Many teams are struggling with this notion because it's not well defined.

The simplistic definition says that students with disabilities are expected to learn the same things that students without disabilities learn. A more reasonable explanation is that all students are entitled to the *opportunity to learn* the same core curriculum. Think about it this way: some students learn advanced physics, but not all do. Yet, *all* students have the opportunity to learn basic principles of physics in science and math classes. A student with significant cognitive delays should have the opportunity to learn the principles of physics, for example, by recognizing and responding to light and sound (forms of energy) and moving objects (matter).

## Planning for Inclusion

Team planning for students with severe needs is a challenge. There are four concepts to keep in mind as a guide:

1. Use state standards, modified as necessary, to develop educationally relevant IEP goals and objectives or benchmarks.

2. Select the five or six main content targets for each unit you teach as the "core curriculum" for your students with severe disabilities.

3. If your students can't perform the entire task or skill, decide how they can do part of it (see "Partial Participation" on the previous page).

4. Match students' daily schedules with their IEP learning expectations and your core curriculum.

**Core curriculum.** Some districts have created a core curriculum that includes the main concepts taught in each subject area. You might need to develop your own. Start by listing the five or six content targets for each unit you teach. (e.g., the five main things students should know about explorers in 2nd grade, or the six major points students should learn about rocks and minerals in 5th grade). Then decide how you'll assess whether your students have learned at least the core curriculum. This "core" should reflect the broad areas of knowledge and experiences expected of all students.

**Sequence of the day.** Using your core curriculum concepts as a base, you can plan more easily for students with severe disabilities. Here are six steps for planning using a "Sequence of the Day" approach:

1. Start with the measurable learning outcomes in your student's IEP. If you follow the guidelines in Chapter 4, your student's IEP goals and objectives or benchmarks will be meaningful for your planning.

2. Plan out the sequence of an average day based on the general education classroom's schedule. (e.g., small group reading, music class, mathematics).

# Sequence-of-the-Day Planning Sheet

**Student:** Theresa K.          **Grade/Subject:** 1st

**Date:** _____          **Teacher** Ms. Smith

The purpose of this planning sheet is to help the teacher organize instruction so that a student's IEP goals and objectives can be infused into class activities, even if that student is not working on exactly the same level as the other students in the class.

| Sequence of the Day | IEP GOALS, OBJECTIVES, AND BENCHMARKS | | | | | | |
|---|---|---|---|---|---|---|---|
| | Given verbal cue, T. will answer "Wh" questions | Given written information at her level, T. will state 2–4 sentence summary | Given verbal or text information, T. will make a prediction of what comes next | Given a 20 min. group activity, T. will work in a cooperative manner | Given 5 opportunities, T. will initiate verbal interactions | Given pictures or manipulatives, T. will state comparisons | Given a model, T. will imitate vocal or gross motor acts |
| **Opening Exercises** | During attendance, T. will answer 4/5 what, who questions | | During lunch count, T. will answer 4/5 prediction questions | | During lunch count, T. states her lunch choice | | |
| **Reading** | T. answers 4/5 who, what, where questions | After story, T. summarizes main idea with 90% accuracy | Periodically, T. answers what happens next with 90% accuracy | T. will work cooperatively for 4/5 days | Given visual cue, T. will interact verbally 3/5 days | T. states which object is bigger or smaller | |
| **Math** | T. answers 4/5 who, what, where, when questions | After example, T. summarizes problem with 80% accuracy | After example, T. answers what will come next with 80% accuracy | T. will work cooperatively for 4/5 days | Given visual cue, T. will interact verbally 3/5 days | T. states which object is hard or soft | T. imitates action with object with 90% accuracy |
| **Music** | T. answers 4/5 who, what, and what doing questions | | | T. will work cooperatively for 4/5 days | Given visual cue, T. will interact verbally 3/5 days | | During song, T. imitates actions with 90% accuracy |

3. Match the IEP goals and objectives or benchmarks with the core curriculum and the times in the day when they can be infused into classroom activities (e.g., If you're doing a class unit on various forms of poetry, and a student with severe disabilities has an IEP objective to identify rhyming words, he or she could find and list all the rhyming words in a given poem).

4. Decide what accommodations are necessary.

5. Be sure to include how your student's performance will be assessed.

6. Determine if any goals, objectives, or benchmarks are missing. If so, revise the schedule, or include time for individual specialized instruction or a small group session.

Team members, such as specialists and para-educators, can work with your student individually and in small group sessions to introduce or reinforce certain skills. (See *Tool 3.2 on page 51: the Sequence-of-the-Day Planning Sheet shows how one team planned for Theresa, a first grade student with autism.*)

## Transition Planning

"Transition" in IDEA usually refers to preparing students for the post-high school years. But transitioning can occur throughout a student's school career, especially when the student moves from one phase of schooling to the next. Helping your students and their families prepare and move to the next stage takes special considerations.

**Birth-to-three enter preschool.** Every state now provides special education services for children with disabilities from birth through 21 years of age. The youngest children, from birth to age two, have an Individualized Family Service Plan (IFSP) instead of an IEP. The process begins with a referral that usually comes from the parent, an early childhood program, or the child's physician. After the child is evaluated, the team and the family write the IFSP. Rather than emphasizing a "general education classroom environment," the IFSP talks about the "natural environment," which might include the home and other community programs where children

without disabilities play and interact (e.g., play groups, child care centers). In many cases, agencies outside of the school district provide the services.

School districts become involved as the child transitions into school-based services or preschool special education programs around age three. The move from birth-to-three services to preschool can be a big step. Parents can get accustomed to having all the support services in their home, which might not continue after age three. Also, the focus now begins to shift from help for the family to direct support for the child. This should be done smoothly to be effective. Your team must have highly tuned interpersonal skills to help families and their "little ones" move from the comfort of home to the world of "school."

**Preschoolers Come to Kindergarten.** Services for a child between the ages of three and five are usually provided in a community preschool, Headstart class, childcare center, or school-based preschool special education classroom. School staff may work directly with the preschool child with disabilities or provide consultation to the staff in the community setting. While your team may write either an IFSP or an IEP, the focus of the activities must be age appropriate. As the child approaches kindergarten age, transitioning is again an important component. The child's family may need to make decisions about the length of his or her school day, different school sites, or program models. They're leaving the comfort of a program they know to participate in one that's unfamiliar. Again, if you're a member of the preschool team, you'll need strong interpersonal skills to help the family gently wade through all of the changes that occur between the preschool environment and the general education elementary school setting.

**Moving to the "big" school.** School districts frequently have different school configurations: primary schools, elementary schools, intermediate schools, middle schools, junior high schools, and high schools. Effective transitioning between each school level is important for all students, especially those with disabilities. Many districts now set up transition IEP meetings to help students move smoothly from one school to another. These don't need to be separate from the regular IEP meeting. Staff members from the sending school, who know the student, exchange personal knowledge with representatives from the receiving school at the student's annual IEP meeting. In turn, receiving school staff members, who know their curriculum and scheduling system, can help the IEP team make better choices about your student's program for the following year. Whichever team you're on, you have important information to share. If you also understand that the family has concerns about leaving behind what they know and moving on to the unknown, you can help them make the transition with less stress and anxiety.

**Planning for life after school.** As your student heads toward adulthood, you, the student, and his or her family need to seek answers to many serious questions: *What will he or she do after high school graduation? Go to college? Have the skills to work in a job? Leave home and live independently? What are your student's desires, interests, and life goals?* Success

after school depends on early, thoughtful, coordinated, and systematic planning.

IDEA asked IEP teams to begin looking into students' *transition service* needs starting at age 14. To participate in transition planning, a student will be invited to the IEP meeting. At this point, your team should focus on your student's curriculum and coursework. What are your student's preferences and interests? How well can your student advocate for himself or herself in making life decisions? Are there career counseling services available in your school?

Preparing your student for the transition IEP meeting is an important first step. Help your student understand the nature of her disability so she's not uncomfortable or upset when it's mentioned. Make sure your student feels actively involved at the meeting. Discuss what coursework would be helpful in career planning. While it's not necessary to write a separate transition plan, IEP goals should begin to focus on the skills your student will need after leaving school. You should include an IEP goal related to career awareness.

Beginning at age 16, transition services should be provided to your student. Good transition services are a coordinated set of activities based on your student's needs, taking into account his or her preferences and interests. To assist with connections to postsecondary services and the community, your student's IEP team will now include a transition specialist, vocational training teacher, or a representative from a transition service agency. Transition services could include linkages to higher education or employment training,

## WHO'S ON THE IEP TEAM

All team members must share responsibility for helping your students meet success. IDEA stated that the IEP team should include the following members:

1. Parents.

2. Regular education teacher (at least one).

3. Special education teacher.

4. Individual who can interpret evaluation results (e.g., school psychologist, speech-language pathologist).

5. Individual representing the school system (e.g., administrator).

6. Individuals with knowledge or special expertise about the child (e.g., an advocate or professional who knows the student and is invited by the parents, or a paraeducator, occupational therapist, physical therapist, or social worker invited, as appropriate, by the school district).

7. Transition service representative, as appropriate.

8. Student, as appropriate. If transition services are to be discussed, the student must be invited.

independent living assistance, or work experiences in the community. You should help the team assess your student's needs and preferences and design an IEP that aligns with post-school goals.

## Make Teaming Work

The collaborative team process doesn't exist in a vacuum. Building a climate of collaboration takes time and commitment from many levels in the school district. Here are some crucial elements of support:

**Shared ownership.** Start with a common mission to educate all students. All team members must share responsibility for helping a student meet success.

**Communication.** Everyone on your team should know and understand his or her responsibilities and be accessible to other team members. Regular, easy vehicles for sharing information need to be in place. Whether it's through face-to-face meetings, E-mail, notes, shared logs, or phone calls, communication must be clear and open.

**Time.** Finding adequate time for your team to plan and collaborate is critical to making it work. Yet, it's the one concern that general and special education teachers raise most often. There never seems to be sufficient time. Your team probably needs a minimum of 45 minutes of uninterrupted planning time each week to be successful. Strategies to make time available include:

1. Use substitutes one day or a half-day every six to eight weeks to allow collaborative instructional teams to extensively plan and discuss students' progress.

2. Block schedule special area classes to permit extended time slots when grade levels can meet to coordinate planning with special education staff members.

3. Work to decrease the unnecessary paperwork you and your team members may be doing to "find" more time in your weekly schedule.

4. Write collaboration time into your student's IEP as a support for personnel.

5. When you do meet, stay focused. Socialize later.

**Reasonable class size and workload.** Staffing patterns must be reasonable. Good collaboration becomes nearly impossible when special education staff members are responsible for too many students or classrooms. Likewise, when general education class sizes are too large, classroom management may take a higher priority than innovative instruction. You can help everyone on your team by working for district policies or contract language that outline reasonable class sizes for general education classes and reasonable caseload/workload limits, or staffing ratios, for special education staff members.

**Think universal design.** When choosing curriculum, ordering materials for the classroom or media center, or renovating or building new schools, we need to consider the needs of students with disabilities. If all the resources you use in your classroom have built-in adaptations for students with learning disabilities or sensory disorders, such as visual or hearing impairments, you could save a lot of time you now spend on adapting instructional materials.

**Professional development.** You can write your training needs into your student's IEP. Collaborative instructional teams need professional development in several areas to be effective, including collaborative decision-making skills. One of the best forms of professional development—technical assistance involving on-site coaching from "experts" in the field—can be part of the personnel supports in your student's IEP. Don't forget to include those "forgotten team members" in the professional development your team receives.

**Administrative support.** Underscoring all the above elements is the support of your administrator. The administrator has the authority and the responsibility to see to it that your class sizes are reasonable and that you have time to plan. He or she can promote your team's efforts or destroy it. An enlightened administrator sees the benefits of the collaborative team process and does everything possible to make it work.

**Parents.** Parents can be your strongest allies in getting the supports you need to make your team efforts a success. They can often advocate for something at the IEP meeting when you can't. If your concerns are focused on your student's needs, the parents may ask to help.

## Why Should I Work with the Team?

It might seem easier to continue to work in isolation but the benefits of the collaborative team process are truly worthwhile.

**You benefit.** The support system of a good collaborative team is energizing for veteran teachers and enriching for newer teachers. Many teachers who have worked on collaborative teams believe it's the best professional development you can get. You'll expand your knowledge of student needs and learn new teaching strategies that you'll use over and over again in coming years.

**Your students benefit.** Students with disabilities gain the opportunity to make friends and to learn from a variety of professional perspectives. Research now tells us that even the students who aren't disabled benefit when students with disabilities are included in their classes. They'll learn to accept other's differences and build friendships with students whom they otherwise might not ever meet. They'll also benefit from your improved teaching skills and from working with different teachers and instructional staff.

# 4 Developing Educationally Relevant IEPs

*"You got to be careful if you don't know where you're going, because you might not get there."*

Yogi Berra

If your student is found to be eligible for special education or *related services,* the IEP team develops an Individualized Education Program (IEP). Ideally, this IEP is the "road map" teachers will use to guide their decisions about a student's instruction. The IEP tells everyone working with a student "where he or she is going" by identifying *annual goals, short-term objectives,* and *benchmarks.* If these goals and objectives are poorly developed, your student may not make the amount of progress everyone is expecting, or the team may not be able to figure out exactly how much progress is being made.

This chapter will discuss ways you and the IEP team can develop meaningful IEPs that are understandable to parents and are relevant "road maps" for classroom instruction.

## Your Role in Writing IEPs

Since a fundamental assumption of IDEA is that students with disabilities should have access to the general education curriculum, the underlying framework for IEP goals and objectives must be the state or local curriculum expectations established for *all* students. That's why it's more critical than ever that educators use a collaborative team process to develop IEPs. General and special education teachers bring different areas of expertise to the table. They need to work with each other to write an effective, meaningful IEP that contains all the ingredients a student needs to get an education that's truly appropriate.

### General Education Teachers

As the content specialist, the general education classroom teacher plays an essential role in developing a student's IEP. You have the knowledge base about the local or state

Chapter 4          Toolkit

**Tool 4.1**
Sample Format for Writing Goals, Objectives, and Benchmarks

**Tool 4.2**
100 Active Verbs for Writing Goals, Objectives, and Benchmarks

standards and the curriculum expectations for your grade level or subject area. You can help the team write classroom-oriented goals and objectives that are relevant to curriculum expectations and related to your classroom-based assessments (CBAs). You can also suggest supplementary aids, services, or other supports that will help you do your job and help your student be successful. As a matter of fact, it's important to get the supports you need written into the IEP.

### Special Educators

Most likely, whether you're the special education teacher or a specialist—such as a speech-language pathologist or an occupational therapist—you'll be involved in helping the team write IEP goals. You have expertise in how students learn and how to individualize instruction based on a student's strengths and needs. You can suggest instructional strategies and ways to modify materials or the classroom environment. You can also help the team write goals and objectives that are specific, measurable, and focused on priority areas.

## How To Write Goals, Objectives, and Benchmarks

The heart of writing any IEP is developing annual goals that describe the desired learning outcomes for a student. Use the following definitions to help you identify the goals, objectives, and benchmarks you want in the IEP:

**Annual goals.** An estimate of what outcomes you can reasonably expect in an academic year based on your student's present levels of performance. Goals may address a student's academic, social, or behavioral needs. Annual goals are broken down into short-term objectives and/or benchmarks.

**Short-term objectives.** Intermediate steps that represent discrete skills your student will learn as he or she progresses toward meeting the annual goal. For example, a short-term math objective might address the ability to do single-digit addition and the next skill might target double-digit addition without carrying.

**Benchmarks.** Also intermediate steps but they represent milestones your student is expected to achieve within a specific period of time. For instance, a reading benchmark might state that your student will read a beginning third grade passage of 100 words by November, while the annual reading goal expects your student to read an end-of-third grade passage of 100 words by June.

### Important Characteristics To Keep in Mind

In the past, IEP goals and objectives were often vague statements, or they included technical terminology that was difficult to understand. Today's IEP goals, objectives, and benchmarks are:

**Specific.** Identify a specific skill, task, behavior, or learning outcome for your student.

**Measurable.** Include a stated method for assessing your student's progress.

**Based on data.** Use your student's present levels of performance as a starting point.

IDEA stated that IEPs must contain information regarding:

1. Student's present levels of performance, including a statement of how the student's disability affects his or her involvement in the general education curriculum.

2. Consideration of the strengths of the student and the parent's concerns for the student's education.

3. Special education or related services that will be provided to the student or on behalf of the student, when they'll begin, how often they'll be provided, where they'll be provided, and how long they will last.

4. Supplementary aids, services, program modifications, or supports for school personnel that will be needed to assist the student.

5. Extent to which the student will *not* participate with nondisabled students.

6. Modifications in test administration the student will need to participate in state- and district-wide assessments, or the reason why the test is not appropriate for this student and a statement about what alternative assessment will be used.

7. Courses (beginning at age 14) the student needs to reach his or her post-school goals and transitional services (beginning at age 16) the student needs to move from high school to post-school activities (e.g., college, vocational training, employment, and independent living).

8. Measurable annual goals, including short-term objectives or benchmarks.

9. How the student's parents will be informed of his or her progress.

**Attainable.** Define a set time period during which your student will achieve the goal (usually within an academic year).

**Relevant.** Relate the IEP goals for your student to the general education curriculum and the established local or state standards for all students.

**Classroom-oriented.** Target skills that can be demonstrated in the classroom, not in a therapeutic setting.

**Focused.** Identify priority areas or learning outcomes for this specific student; don't list the entire curriculum.

**Shared.** Reflect the importance of all team members working from a common understanding of your student's needs toward a shared plan.

# Using State or Local Standards

State or local student expectations are usually referred to as either content standards or performance standards. You or someone on the IEP team should be familiar with your district's standards.

## Selecting Content Standards

Many school districts have convened committees to develop a bank of IEP goals, objectives, and benchmarks that are based on state or local standards. In the absence of such models in your district, you and your team could draw up your own schema for writing standards-based goals, objectives, and benchmarks.

## Selecting Standards for Social and Behavior Skills

If your student has behavior problems, but they don't affect his or her academic progress, that student may not qualify for special education. But if you do write an IEP for a student with behavior problems, you may need to focus the annual goals on his or her social and behavioral skills. Your state standards may not include a specific section that outlines social and behavior expectations.

However, you can use other content areas—such as health and safety, character education, or social studies—that address risk-taking behaviors, work ethic, citizenship, and social relationships.

## Steps for Writing Goals from Standards

*Take a look at the sidebar on page 61, Sample Goal Written from a State Standard.* You'll see the steps that were used to write Jonathan's annual goal. Consider the following steps as you write the annual goals for your student:

**Define present levels of performance.** Your student's present levels of performance are your starting point. By pooling the information gained from your CBAs and the results of multidisciplinary team evaluations, you'll have a rich description of your student's present levels of performance. *What standards has your student achieved already?*

**Consider family concerns.** Explore life goals with your student's family. *Do they anticipate their child living independently after leaving school? Do they want their child to go into the family business? Do they expect him/her to attend college?*

**Prioritize skill areas.** Establish the priority areas for your student. Based on your student's identified disability, some standards may be more difficult to meet than others without special instruction and support. They should be part of your priorities. You don't need to address all of the state or district standards. Nor do you have to write goals in all curriculum areas. *What skill areas, if enhanced, could make the greatest difference for* your student? Which standards are prerequisites for later skill development?

**Gauge progress.** Estimate the amount of progress your student might make in an academic year. *What do you know about your student's learning rate, strengths, and motivation?*

**Decide on priority goals.** Select the annual goal(s) from among the state or district standards that are priorities for your student. *Are these important? Are they attainable?*

**Modify standards, if needed.** Decide if your student can meet the entire standard(s), part of the standard(s) or a modified version of the standard(s). *Does your student partially meet the standard already but needs to complete it fully* before moving on to a different standard? If modified, would the standard be an appropriate goal for a student with severe disabilities?

**List accommodations.** Describe any conditions, supports, or accommodations the student might need to meet the standard(s). *Does the student need an assistance device, sign language, prompt, or cueing system?*

**Measure progress.** Explain how you'll determine whether the goal has been achieved. *How will you measure progress?*

**Describe competence.** Define what level of competence you expect. *When will you know that your student has reached this goal?*

## SAMPLE GOAL WRITTEN FROM A STATE STANDARD

**Present Level of Performance:** Jonathan is a sixth grade student who has an identified learning disability that interferes with his ability to understand math concepts and spatial relationships. He can add, subtract, multiply, and divide double digits with whole numbers and can describe simple ratios. Jonathan is on grade level in reading. His family hopes that he'll be able to attend college.

**State Standard:** Students will use ratios, proportions, and percents to represent relationships between quantities and measures and solve problems involving ratios, proportions, and percents.

**Priority Areas for Jonathan:** Using relationships between quantities and measurements to do math problem solving. Concept development for algebraic and geometric problem solving.

**Annual Goal:** By June, Jonathan will apply ratios, proportions, and percents to solve 20 written math problems with 90 percent accuracy on three consecutive weekly assignments.

# Making IEPs Measurable

IDEA states that IEP annual goals, objectives, and benchmarks must be measurable. If you've never written measurable learning outcomes, this might seem like a formidable task. There are ways to simplify the job.

## Four Components of Goals, Objectives, and Benchmarks

Whether you're writing goals, objectives, or benchmarks, you should include the following four components. *(Also, see Tool 4.1 on page 63: Sample Format for Writing Goals, Objectives, and Benchmarks, and Tool 4.2 on page 65: 100 Active Verbs for Writing Goals, Objectives, and Benchmarks.)*

**Task.** What specific task, skill, behavior, or learning outcome do I want my student to accomplish? *(Jonathan will use ratios, proportions, and percents to solve word problems.)*

**Conditions.** How is my student going to show that he can do this task? Include a clear description of the material you'll use to assess the task or skill. *(Jonathan will complete 20 written word problems on weekly assignments.)* You can also define the type of response expected *(Given a multiple-choice format, Jonathan will . . .),* or you can define the setting. *(Given the classroom setting, Jonathan will . . .).*

**Accommodations.** What accommodations are needed, if any? These are the adaptations that are provided for both instruction and assessment. You can add an accommodation involving time *(given extended time)* or technology *(given a calculator)* to Jonathan's annual goal.

**Performance Criteria.** How and when are you going to measure achievement? *(By June, . . . with 90 percent accuracy on three consecutive weekly assignments.)*

## How To Write Performance Criteria

Writing clear *performance criteria* in any learning outcome is key to making your IEPs measurable. You'll be responsible for using whatever performance criteria you list to monitor and report on your student's progress throughout the year. Your performance criteria should have four parts:

**Criterion level.** The criterion level is the level of mastery you expect. It's often written in terms of percentage correct (90 percent accuracy) or the number of trials correct (4 out of 5 times). Since most of us are not math wizards, it's easiest to use a base of 10 or 5 trials for your percentages. In other words, you give your student 5 or 10 or 20 opportunities to demonstrate his or her skill at the task. Then, you can quickly calculate the accuracy level (4 correct out of 5 trials = 80 percent; 6 correct out of 10 trials = 60 percent; 15 correct out of 20 trials = 75 percent). Remember from our discussion in Chapter 2 that your expectations for mastery should be reasonable. A certain margin of error is acceptable. Satisfactory accuracy of a learning outcome is usually at the 80–90 percent level.

**Consistency.** Consistency means the number of times you expect a student to demonstrate competence before you consider the skill to be mastered. Usually a student is expected to perform at the expected accuracy level at least three consecutive times.

# Sample Format for Writing Goals, Objectives, and Benchmarks

**Consider the formula below for writing goals, objectives, and benchmarks for your student:**

**Condition + Accommodation + Student's Name + Skill/Task/Behavior + Performance Criteria**

## Example A

Given at least five opportunities during classroom discussions to ask questions and make comments, and one verbal prompt from the teacher, Dan will raise his hand and respond when acknowledged with 90 percent accuracy on three consecutive days.

## Example B

By June, when given a fourth grade level writing prompt and extended time, Chris will compose a written response of at least three paragraphs expressing clear meaning, internal structure, organization, correct syntax, and spelling with 90 percent accuracy on three consecutive weekly assignments.

## Examples of Conditions

- Given a random selection of 20 words from a pool of 100 words
- Given a fourth grade reading passage
- Given a worksheet of 10 examples/problems
- Given five opportunities to do X (a specific task)
- Given the weekly spelling test
- Given an end-of-term multiple choice test format/true-false test format
- Given a sixth grade level writing prompt
- Given a group activity of 20 minutes
- Given the classroom setting

## Examples of Accommodations

- Braillewriter
- Signed translation
- Communication device
- Picture exchange board
- Scanner
- Reader
- Large print display
- Slant board
- Calculator
- Spell checker
- Repeated instructions
- Audiotape recorded instructions
- Highlighted key words in a written passage
- Colored acetate
- Visual, verbal, physical prompting
- Extended time
- Individual carrel

**Frequency.** Frequency refers to the interval you use to assess the learning outcome. It might be daily, twice a week, weekly, or on another type of timetable related to your class or school calendar. Use a frequency that fits easily into your planning and your student's schedule. Consider any assessments that are part of the curriculum (e.g., end-of-book quizzes, weekly spelling tests, midterm exams).

**Mastery date.** The previous three components can be used with annual goals, objectives, and benchmarks. Mastery dates, however, apply most appropriately to annual goals and benchmarks because they mark time (e.g., by January, by June).

### How To Break Down Goals into Objectives

There are two ways to segment the annual goal into objectives or benchmarks:

**Discrete skills.** It's easier to divide some goals into the separate skills. This approach is especially effective for segmenting written language, social, behavioral, study, and independent living skills. For example, to accomplish a written language goal, your student might need to learn elements of organization, elaboration, and structure.

**Sequential.** Most goals logically break down into sequential phases. For instance, you teach reading and math using increasing steps of difficulty. Also, you can sequence discrete skills that aren't learned in any particular order by decreasing the accommodations or prompting you provide (e.g., First your student does a task with the help of a physical prompt, then only with the help of a verbal cue).

### How Many Objectives or Benchmarks Should You Write?

Remember that the IEP does not have to represent your entire curriculum. Every step in the process of accomplishing a goal does not need to become an objective or a benchmark. IEP annual goals are the priority areas for the student. Objectives or benchmarks should be those single gains toward the goal that will best show parents and other team members that your student is making progress and is likely to achieve the goal.

To help you decide how many objectives or benchmarks to write, keep these points in mind:

**Progress report dates.** IDEA says that you must inform your student's family of his or her progress at least as often as the families of students without disabilities are told of their children's progress. If your district requires you to do progress reports three or four times a year, it might be best to break your annual goal into three or four objectives or benchmarks.

**Prioritizing.** If there seems to be an overwhelming number of objectives or benchmarks for a particular goal, the IEP team should consider prioritizing them and selecting those that will demonstrate progress in the most meaningful way for parents.

**Team support.** When your team writes shared goals, several team members are assigned the task of charting growth. This requires good communication strategies among team members, and it reduces the responsibility that any one person has in measuring and reporting progress.

# 100 Active Verbs for Writing Goals, Objectives, and Benchmarks

Here are 100 active verbs you can use to write observable and measurable student expectations
(e.g., target behaviors, goals, objectives, benchmarks).

| | | |
|---|---|---|
| add | diagram | operate |
| analyze | differentiate | organize |
| apply | differentiate between | pick |
| appraise | discriminate | plan |
| arrange | discuss | predict |
| assemble | distinguish | prepare |
| calculate | divide | present |
| categorize | dramatize | produce |
| choose | draw conclusions | propose |
| cite examples of | employ | question |
| collect | engage in | read |
| communicate | estimate | recall |
| compare | evaluate | recognize |
| complete | examine | reconstruct |
| compose | experiment | record |
| conclude | explain | relate |
| construct | express | repeat |
| contrast | follow directions | report |
| correlate | formulate | respond |
| copy | identify | restate |
| create | illustrate | review |
| criticize | imitate | select |
| debate | infer | sequence |
| deduce | initiate | solve |
| define | inspect | spell |
| demonstrate | interact | state |
| demonstrate use of | interpret | subtract |
| describe | list | tell |
| design | locate | translate |
| detect | manage | underline |
| determine | modify | use |
| develop | multiply | utilize |
| devise | name | write |
| diagnose | | |

## Meeting IEP Expectations

The achievement of IEP goals is not guaranteed. These goals are estimates of a student's progress based on your best professional judgment. By periodically reporting on progress during the year, parents and team members can gauge whether or not a student is making enough growth to reasonably meet the annual goals. If you don't see adequate progress, it might be time to meet with the parents and revise your student's IEP expectations.

To develop educationally relevant IEPs:

1. IEP expectations must align with the standards and curriculum expectations that exist for students who are not disabled.

2. IEP goals, objectives, and benchmarks must be understandable to parents, students, and other educators.

3. IEP goals, objectives, and benchmarks must be measurable so that parents and other educators can use them to monitor the student's progress during the year.

# Making Accommodations and Modifications

*"I get by with a little help from my friends. Gonna try with a little help from my friends."*

The Beatles

All teachers use varying kinds of instructional strategies and adaptations to help students with diverse needs in their classrooms. We all know that some students need more help than others. We also know that identifying *accommodations* and *modifications* for students with disabilities is allowed, in fact is required, by IDEA.

The notion that students with disabilities need a "little help" to participate successfully in the general education curriculum is not a new one. But many teachers are finding that the accommodations they use with students with disabilities are also useful strategies to use with other students in their classrooms.

This chapter will suggest guidelines for deciding what adaptations struggling students need to help them learn and students with disabilities need to access the general education environment. We'll also discuss how your team can incorporate accommodations and modifications into your collaborative instruction.

## A Continuum of Support

All collaborative instructional team members should be aware of what adaptations a student needs to be successful. If your student has an IEP, the IEP team will list necessary accommodations and modifications in the IEP. However, these terms are often used differently or interchangeably from state to state, or even from school to school.

Accommodations and modifications actually exist along a continuum of educational supports. Many teachers automatically use

### Chapter 5

**Tool 5.1**
Accommodations and Modifications
Planning Worksheet

**Tool 5.2**
Accommodations and Modifications
Checklist

**Tool 5.3**
Accommodations and Modifications
Assessment Checklist

accommodations and view these techniques as just "good teaching," such as writing key words on the board. Teachers often use accommodations with diverse learners, such as students who have *504 Accommodation Plans* and those who are English language learners. During the intervention process, you may have tried some of these accommodations as *alternative strategies.*

On the other hand, instructional modifications go beyond accommodations. They are alterations in the curriculum content, type of instruction, or materials. There are varying opinions from state to state about what constitutes a modification. In some states, significant adjustments beyond accommodations are called "alternate instruction." For our purposes, we'll view modifications as those changes most likely to impact learning outcomes for your student, so that he or she is learning different material, only part of the curriculum, or at a much slower pace. You normally use modifications only with those students who have significant academic problems.

## A Word About Fairness

Teachers often ask if it's fair to offer accommodations and modifications to a student with a disability but not to other students. These adaptations are not provided to guarantee your student success. They allow a level playing field so that students with disabilities have the same *opportunity* to succeed as their nondisabled peers. It's a chance to participate, not an advantage. In this context, "fair" does not mean equal treatment; it means equity. Each student receives what he or she needs to have an opportunity to succeed.

## Principles for Selection

As you decide what accommodations or modifications are appropriate for your student, keep these five principles in mind:

**Don't assume.** Don't assume that all students with disabilities need accommodations and modifications. Some don't. Some need them in one situation but not another.

**Be consistent.** Use the same accommodations and modifications for instruction you use for assessment. If you use an adaptation during testing but not during instruction, it might confuse your student and affect his or her performance on the assessment.

**Individualize.** Base your decision on what supports a particular student needs, not on what other students receive.

**Use the approved list.** Check to see if your state or district has a list of approved accommodations and modifications, especially for assessments.

**Build independence.** Reassess your student's need for an adaptation, at least annually. While some supports may always be necessary, you should encourage as much independence as possible. Wean your student from the accommodation or modification as soon as he or she is able to manage without it.

*(See Tool 5.1 on page 69: the Accommodations and Modifications Planning Worksheet shows how your team can communicate about what adaptations are needed for your student at different points in the day.)*

# Accommodations and Modifications
# Planning Worksheet

**Student:**  Lori W.                          **Grade:**  2nd grade

**Date:**                                       **Teacher:**  Ms. Thomas

| Time | Activity and Accommodation or Modification | Level of Participation | Implementer(s) |
|---|---|---|---|
| 8:00 – 8:30 | **Start-Up** | | |
| | AM check-in to organize day | F | Ms. Thomas & Ms. Robinson |
| | Extra time to organize materials | | (paraeducator) |
| | Review of Sequence-of-the-Day chart | | |
| 8:30 – 9:00 | **Reading group** | P | |
| | Seat near teacher | | Ms. Thomas |
| | Display key vocabulary | | Ms. Thomas |
| | Student's word bank | | Ms. Robinson |
| | Prompt to stay on task | | Ms. Robinson |
| 9:00 – 9:30 | **Independent work at desk** | F | |
| | Highlight instructions with marker | | Ms. Robinson |
| | Use raised-line paper and large type | | Ms. Robinson |
| | Permit break after 10 minutes of work | | Ms. Robinson |
| | Checklist for completed work on desk | | Ms. Robinson |
| 9:30 – 10:00 | **Physical Education Class** | P | |
| | Define space for Lori in room | | Mr. Potter & Ms. Robinson |
| | Stand near student when giving directions | | |
| | Review and display behavioral rules | | |
| | Provide "wait" time for response | | |
| | Implement behavioral contract and rewards | | |

Note: Level of Participation  P = Partial;  F = Full

# Accommodations

Accommodations change how you structure the environment, how you present material, or how you allow students to respond to the material. You can use them in many, if not all, learning environments, including special area classes. Sometimes a student's IEP identifies certain accommodations for nonacademic and extracurricular activities as well (e.g., recess, field trips, after-school events).

## Accommodations for Instruction

Take a look at the following suggestions to see how you can indicate what instructional accommodations your student might need to be successful. *(Also see Tool 5.2, the Accommodations and Modifications Checklist, on page 71.)*

**Environment.** Altering the setting, or how you structure your class, can be a minimal change for you but significant for some students. These changes could include:

- Preferential seating.

- Physical change in room arrangement.

- Defined physical space for the student within the room.

- Specifically stated behavioral rules and consequences.

- Minimized visual or auditory distractions (e.g., noise buffers).

- Use of special lighting.

- Daily schedule displayed to aid in transitions.

- Adaptive furniture.

**Presentation.** Changes in how you present instruction could involve:

- Pace or time adjustments (e.g., one assignment at a time, time extensions to complete work, or frequent breaks).

- Multisensory presentation techniques (e.g., taped lectures to allow for replay, use of graphic organizers, sign language interpreter or visual models for a student who is deaf or hearing impaired).

- Assistive technology (e.g., highlighted key vocabulary, spellchecker, calculator, color overlay, Braille text, visual magnifying equipment).

- Reinforcements (e.g., positive feedback, stickers, repeated directions, peer tutors, study guides, or periodic comprehension checks).

**Response mode.** Take advantage of your student's preferences and strengths when selecting response modes. Response accommodations may be defined by:

- Type (e.g., allow oral rather than written responses; permit recorded, dictated, or typed answers; let your student copy from a book; apply no spelling penalty; or use a communication device).

- Length (e.g., break an assignment into smaller parts, or reduce the number of paper/pencil tasks).

# Accommodations and Modifications Checklist

This checklist is marked to indicate the needs of Gail, a student who is disorganized and easily distracted.

**Student:** _Gail L._         **Teacher:** _Mr. Walker_

**Date:** _____ **Grade:** _8th_

### ENVIRONMENT OR SETTING
- ☐ Seat near teacher
- ☑ Assign student to low-distraction area
- ☑ Seat near positive peer models
- ☐ Use study carrel
- ☐ Use of time-out
- ☐ Define physical space for student within the room
- ☑ Stand near student when giving instructions
- ☐ Display specific behavioral rules
- ☐ Special lighting

### PRESENTATION
- ☐ Use visual aids with oral presentation
- ☑ Display key vocabulary
- ☐ Use multisensory presentation
- ☐ Use concrete or personalized examples
- ☑ Provide models
- ☑ Course outlines or study guides
- ☑ Highlight instructions (marker or highlighter tape)
- ☐ Use markers or organizers to keep place
- ☑ Repeat directions
- ☑ Student to repeat instructions for comprehension
- ☐ Use mnemonics
- ☐ Provide student with vocabulary word bank
- ☐ Use motivational game-like materials
- ☐ Call on student often
- ☑ Acknowledge effort
- ☑ Prompt student to stay on task
- ☑ Provide additional prompts & cues as needed
- ☐ Use dark ink or raised lines
- ☐ Use increased spacing between items on page
- ☐ Use buff-colored rather than white paper
- ☐ Provide prompts on audiotape
- ☑ Allow student to tape-record lesson
- ☐ Arrange for a note taker
- ☐ Use sign language interpreter
- ☐ Give student a copy of lecture notes

### PACE, TIME, OR SCHEDULING
- ☐ Permit breaks between tasks
- ☑ Provide "wait" time for responses
- ☐ Display daily schedule
- ☐ Modify student's schedule to fit optimal learning times

### CURRICULUM CONTENT
- ☐ Adjust work load
- ☐ Reduce assignments
- ☐ Simplify number of items presented on page
- ☐ Give alternative assignments in subject
- ☐ Pre-teach content

### RESPONSE MODE
- ☐ Allow oral responses
- ☐ Permit scribe for answers
- ☐ Use pencil grip
- ☐ Use calculator, math tables, or abacus
- ☐ Use spell checker or dictionary
- ☐ Use tape recorder
- ☐ Allow alternate response mode: _____
  (e.g., Braille, picture exchange system, sign language)

### ADAPTED MATERIALS OR EQUIPMENT
- ☐ Use large type/magnifying equipment
- ☐ Keep page format simple
- ☑ Divide page into clearly marked sections
- ☑ Remove distractions from paper
- ☐ Use slant board or wedge
- ☐ Use computer-assisted instruction
- ☐ Use adapted equipment: _____
  (e.g., adapted computer keyboard, augmentative communication device, Braillewriter)

### ORGANIZATIONAL STRATEGIES
- ☑ Training in how to take notes
- ☐ Give one assignment at a time
- ☐ Checklist on desk for work completed
- ☐ Folders to hold work
- ☑ Post assignments
- ☑ Use calendar to plan long-term assignments
- ☑ Use of assignment notebook
- ☐ Give time to organize desk during class
- ☐ AM check-in to organize for the day
- ☐ Lunch time check-in to organize for PM
- ☐ PM check-out to organize for homework
- ☐ Assign homework partner
- ☑ Arrange for duplicate materials to use at home
- ☐ Develop parent/school contract
- ☐ Provide training in time management

### TYPE OF INSTRUCTION
- ☐ Individual or small group instruction
- ☐ Peer tutoring
- ☐ Cross-age tutoring
- ☑ Study-buddy
- ☐ Work with paraeducator
- ☑ Confer with staff during available times
- ☑ Teach student to monitor own behavior
- ☐ Implement behavior contract & reward system
- ☐ Conflict resolution strategies
- ☐ Other: _____

### Accommodations for Assessment

Remember that the same accommodations you use for instruction should be used during assessment. This applies to the daily, weekly, and periodic quizzes and exams you give during the school year. Accommodations used during assessments should not alter what the test measures or interfere in your ability to compare the results a student with disabilities achieved with other students' results. *(See Tool 5.3 on page 73: the Accommodations and Modifications Assessment Checklist demonstrates a quick, easy way to indicate what assessments and modifications your student might need.)* In addition to the instructional accommodations listed previously, your student's adaptations in the testing situation might include:

**Environment or Setting.** Let your student take the test in a separate, quiet room or use a study carrel to reduce distractions; secure the answer booklet to the desk; etc.

**Scheduling.** Administer the test at specific times of the day; administer the test over several days; allow more breaks; or administer the subtests in a different order.

**Presentation.** Shorten the length of the exam; permit more time; allow use of Braille, large print, or sign language; read the test verbatim to your student; reduce the visible print on the page by using a template; provide prompts or cues to focus your student; or allow your student to use an open book or notes to find the answers.

**Response Mode.** Change the test format from fill in the blank to multiple choice; allow oral rather than written answers; enlarge the bubble answer sheet; or use a scribe to record your student's test answers.

## Modifications

Modifications require alterations in the curriculum content, type of instruction, or materials you provide to your student. Students with moderate to severe disabilities, sensory deficits (e.g., deafness, blindness), or more than one disability (e.g., deaf-blind), may need modifications. Your student's IEP team will decide which modifications are appropriate.

### Modifications for Instruction

**Curriculum content.** You may need to modify the curriculum you present to your student. This is accomplished by:

- Reduced content (e.g., present only part of the curriculum, or expect your student only to participate partially in the lesson).

- Simplified content (e.g., use a text that has a reading level commensurate with the student's reading or language level).

- Alternate content (e.g., provide curriculum that is typically not presented to nondisabled peers, such as teaching an older student to use a bus to get to work).

- Shortened assignments (e.g., require your student to write a shorter essay).

# Accommodations and Modifications
# Assessment Checklist

This assessment is marked to indicate the needs of Percy, a student who fatigues quickly and reads significantly below grade level.

**Student:** ___Percy S._____  **Teacher:** ___Mrs. Hyde_____

**Date:**_____  **Grade:** ___10th_____

### ASSESSMENT ACCOMMODATIONS OR MODIFICATIONS

☐ Use short, frequent quizzes
☑ Permit breaks during tests
☑ Permit movement
☐ Reduce number of test items
☐ Limit multiple choice
☑ Preview test procedures
☑ Practice taking similar test questions
☑ Periodic checks for answers marked in correct spaces
☐ Arrange for oral testing
☐ Support staff administers test
☐ Permit student to type or use word processing
☑ Permit untimed testing
☐ Give test over several sessions
☐ Administer test at specific time of day
☑ Administer test in separate setting
☐ Administer using a study carrel
☑ Give prior notice for quizzes
☑ Read test to student
☐ Permit templates to reduce visible print
☐ Rephrase test questions and directions
☐ Allow open book or notes
☐ Increase size of bubbles on answer sheet
☐ Provide cues on answer sheet
☐ Secure answer sheet to work area
☑ Student marks on test booklet
☐ Permit adapted format: _____
☐ Use adapted equipment: _____

### GRADING
☐ Use grading criteria based on individual ability
☐ Base grade on IEP
☐ Adjusted grading option; grade satisfactory/unsatisfactory, credit/no credit
☑ No spelling penalty
☑ No handwriting penalty

**Type of instruction.** In order to help a student with disabilities achieve the learning outcomes in his or her IEP, you may use different instructional strategies than the ones you use with other students. These could be:

- Individual or small group instruction (e.g., service your student in appropriate settings, such as a "pull out," "push-in," or substantially separate class environment).

- Paraeducator support (e.g., assign a one-on-one tutor or aide).

- Specialized instruction (e.g., teach specific skills through an instructional method not typically used with nondisabled peers).

**Materials.** Sometimes your student requires materials that are significantly different from those used with nondisabled peers. These might include:

- Adapted instructional materials (e.g., sequence-of-the-day display boards, picture exchange communication systems, teacher-modified worksheets that reduce or simplify the expected response from a student).

- Adapted equipment (e.g., augmentative communication systems, adaptive computer keyboards).

### Modifications for Assessment

As we discussed under Accommodations, you should use the same modifications for assessment that you use for instruction. However,

modifications, as we've defined them, are rarely allowed for state-wide and district-wide assessments because they tend to alter what the test is measuring. There are a couple of exceptions:

- Adapted equipment (e.g., Students can use a communication device as a response mode).

- Adapted format (e.g., Students can use a different version of the test, such as Braille, large print, or text with fewer items per page for easier reading).

## State-Wide and District-Wide Assessments

IDEA required that all IEP teams determine how, not whether, students with disabilities would participate in state-wide and district-wide assessments. In addition, Section 504 and the American Disabilities Act prohibit excluding students from federally or publicly run programs (such as the standardized assessment program in your school). Plus, when lawmakers passed H.R. 1, No Child Left Behind Act (ESEA), in January 2002, all school districts were required to implement annual large-scale assessments of all students by the 2005–06 school year.

Since students with disabilities can't be totally exempted from taking the general state or school district tests, you and the IEP team have two choices: 1) define what accommodations will be provided for your student when he or she takes the tests, or 2) document why the test is not appropriate for this particular student and how he or she will be tested using an alternate assessment approved by the state or district.

## Alternate Assessments

An alternate assessment is truly different from the assessments that other students take. In most cases, alternate assessments are used only with students who are unable to take the large-scale assessments even with accommodations or modifications. Typically, students who take alternate assessments meet these criteria: 1) their cognitive ability and adaptive behavior prevent them from completing the general education curriculum, even with modifications; and 2) their course of study is primarily functional and life-skill oriented. IDEA required that each state develop a different way to evaluate the progress of these students toward the state or local standards.

If the IEP team decides that your student can't participate in the state-wide and district-wide assessments, you'll still need to evaluate his or her learning progress against state or local standards. Typical alternate assessments include student portfolios, family interviews, teacher observation checklists, or a state-approved standardized alternate assessment instrument.

# 6 Communicating with Parents

*"Always speak the truth—think before you speak—and write it down afterwards."*

The Red Queen advising Alice in
*Through the Looking-Glass* by Lewis Carroll

The Red Queen gave Alice excellent advice during her adventures in Wonderland. Truthful, thoughtful communication is key to working cooperatively with others. And documenting what you've said is always a good idea.

Some educators feel that communicating productively with parents can be more challenging than Alice's trip through Wonderland. Nonetheless, parents are an essential part of your student's "team" and can be your best supporters. You must get them involved and maintain a good relationship with them to ensure your student's success.

Remember, parents can be your strongest partners. They can step forward to advocate for the supports you need to teach their children when you feel powerless to do so yourself. When educators are able to communicate with parents that they share the same central goal—to provide a good education for their children—they win powerful education allies.

This chapter will suggest practical strategies for connecting with your student's parents—those who are "hard to reach" and those who are "hands on."

## Your First Contact

First impressions can have long-lasting effects. The first time you speak with your student's parents, you need to leave a positive impression. It's always in your best interest to develop constructive partnerships with parents. Ultimately, your job as an educator will be easier, and your students will make more progress.

### Chapter 6

**Tool 6.1**
Weekly Homework Log

**Tool 6.2**
Daily Home Report

**Tool 6.3**
Conference Planning Sheet for Parents

Whether it's a planned occasion (e.g., a parent-teacher conference or an IEP meeting) or a chance encounter (e.g., a community event or the school hallway), you should present yourself as warm, open, sensitive, flexible, reliable, and accessible. No one is asking you to pretend you're someone you aren't. Just present your most positive characteristics. These attributes make parents feel most comfortable with teachers, according to researchers.

## Encouraging Parent Support

Researchers also say that those parents who are best able to be supportive partners in their child's education are happy in their marriages, have harmonious family situations, have experienced successful school and parent-teacher relationships in the past, and are generally open to the ideas of others. Unfortunately, due to the complications of today's world, your student's parents may or may not have these life situations. They may feel overwhelmed by the challenges presented by their child's disabilities or pressures in their own lives. They could be single parents who lead very complex lives. Or they might have difficulty engaging in their children's education programs because their own school experiences were negative or unsuccessful. Even with these hurdles, you can still take positive steps to encourage parental support.

### Guidelines for Positive Parent-Teacher Communication

Both parents and teachers share responsibility for fostering positive communication between home and school. You can help your student's parents be constructive partners in their child's education by keeping these guidelines in mind:

**Be accessible.** To start on the right foot, make yourself accessible early. For example, at the beginning of the year or at your first opportunity, explain to your student's parents how and when they can reach you.

**Be positive.** Mention your student's strengths. Too often, teachers only contact parents when their child is having problems. Make the effort to talk to your student's parents about what he or she does well. Try to begin and end discussions on a positive note. Even if the purpose of the conference was to tell parents about a student's difficulties, summarize by making a commitment to work together (e.g., "I'm confident that by working together, we can help your son/daughter do better.")

**Be prompt.** Be on time for a parent conference to show you respect the parents' time and their role in their child's education. Likewise, contact your student's parents promptly when you have concerns or your student begins to have problems. Don't wait until conference time to "spring bad news" on them.

**Be persistent.** If your first attempt to call your student's family is unsuccessful, call again or send home a letter explaining your need to reach them. If you still can't reach them, call the emergency number on their registration card, phone them at work, send a second note home with a neighbor, or ask a related services staff member (e.g., social worker or school psychologist) to make contact for you. Remember to document all of your attempts to reach your student's parents, and make copies of any letters you send home.

**Respect confidentiality.** Your student and his or her family have the right to expect that their personal information is kept private. In fact, there are laws that protect a student's right to confidentiality (i.e., FERPA). Don't talk about a student's home situation or difficulties in the teacher's lounge or at social events. Be careful not to share private information about a student with other parents. Always keep in mind that this could be your child. Ask yourself, "Would I want someone to talk like this about my child?"

**Avoid jargon.** One of the most common complaints from parents is that educators tend to use too much jargon that parents don't understand. They're embarrassed to stop and ask what a term means. Use clear vocabulary that is easily understood by anyone. If you must use a technical term, define it quickly and move on, for example, "Let's talk about your daughter's reading comprehension skills; that's how well she understands what she reads."

**Be specific.** When you discuss a student's problems with parents, be specific about their child's needs. Global statements like, "He never listens" or "She can't do anything in my class" may cause parents to think you don't like their child. They may dismiss your concerns or become defensive.

**Be truthful.** Minimizing your student's difficulties may cause parents to think that it's not very serious, when in fact it is. Later, they could feel you lied to them. Parents may not like what you have to say, but they must know that you shared your concerns and information honestly.

**Use active listening.** To show that you are listening to your student's parents, use active listening techniques. Reflect back to parents the major points they are making, for example, "I understand that you are concerned about his progress or I'm glad to hear that you work on his homework with him." You can also clarify what they are saying to be sure there are no misunderstandings (e.g., "Are you saying that you feel your son is not trying?").

**Use repetition.** Sometimes, parents don't listen well, are resistant, or go on tangents during your conversation. If so, the "broken record" technique can be effective. Restate your need or point repeatedly throughout the discussion. For example, if Russell is consistently tardy to school and his parents offer excuses for him, say "I understand that, but I need Russell to come to school on time." If Russell's parents begin to talk about an unrelated issue, repeat, "I understand you're concerned about that, but I need your son to come to school on time. I want to address his tardiness."

**Avoid "fortune-telling."** Parents are concerned about their child's future. Even if a child is very young, parents may ask you to predict whether their child will go to college or "catch up." It's best to respond frankly that it's difficult to forecast a student's progress because each one is different, with a separate set of skills and circumstances. You can honestly respond, "I don't know." If you feel you must respond "hopefully," you might say: "Many students make good progress with the proper support" or "With your help, I intend to do everything I can to help your daughter do her best."

**Document.** Get into the habit of having someone you trust read over information you're sending home. They can catch spelling and grammar errors you've missed and provide a perspective on your tone. Always date and make copies of letters you send home. If you communicate with a parent through E-mail, print a copy or save it to a file in case you need it later. Many school districts have log forms in student files for parent contacts—use them. After a phone conversation or face-to-face conference, write down the major points you discussed and any solutions you proposed. If you're meeting with a parent whom you expect to be angry or upset, ask a colleague or the principal to sit in on the meeting. You'll have a witness to any comments you make and support if a parent becomes aggressive.

## Understanding Parents' Perspective

Knowing the viewpoint of your student's family can help you prevent misunderstandings and conflicts. Ask them what their opinions are. Listen to them and try to understand their perspective. You don't have to agree with them to recognize what they're saying and how they feel. For many parents, their primary role in their child's life is to be an advocate. You probably believe that you, too, are advocating for what's best for your student. But remember, each of you knows this child in a different context. Because you and the family play different roles in a student's life, you may have different opinions about what's best. In addition, there may be pressures on your student's parents from relatives, neighbors, or other members of their church or community.

**Physical.** If their child was an infant when his or her disabilities were first identified, or if the child has ongoing significant medical problems, the parents may be anxious about what physicians or other health professionals have suggested about the future. They may have been told at birth that their child would never learn to talk or walk and should be institutionalized. For some parents whose children have serious daily health issues, keeping their child alive is a greater priority than school performance.

**Linguistic.** Parents who don't speak or read English can feel alienated in a school environment. Efforts should be made to translate progress reports and other important documents for them. Ideally, an interpreter or bilingual staff member should help you speak personally with them. IDEA required the school to make reasonable efforts to arrange for an interpreter during IEP meetings, particularly when the student's placement is discussed. Your district should take whatever steps are necessary to ensure that your student's parents understand evaluation reports and what is said at IEP meetings.

**Cultural.** The diverse cultural beliefs within our country make up a patchwork of understandings between schools and families. Certain cultures revere the authoritative position of a teacher. As a result, to avoid offending you, your student's parents may not challenge or ask questions of you. In some cultures, an elder relative or educated community member assumes the responsibility of communicating with the school for the family. Relatives should not be dismissed because they're not "legal parents." If they're recent immigrants to this country, your student's parents may be unaware of the supports available through the schools, or they may think they'll have to pay for any additional services their child receives. In some cultures, children with difficulties are considered an embarrassment to the whole family. Or cultural expectations might require that the parents—not the school or society—take responsibility for their child's "weaknesses."

**Economic.** Making a living is sometimes the number one priority for a family. Job pressures can keep parents from participating fully in their children's learning. If your student's parent is single, she or he may be holding down two jobs while trying to keep the family together. Just because parents may not be able to come to school often, or be actively involved in school events, doesn't mean they don't care about their child's education.

## Considerations for Students Without IEPs

If your student is struggling but doesn't have an IEP, his or her problems may be new, or they may be old issues that are gradually worsening over time. You could be the first educator to tell the parents that you're concerned about their child's performance. Being the bearer of difficult news puts you in a tricky position and must be handled carefully. When parents first hear that their child is having academic or behavior problems, it's natural for them to react with fear, disbelief, or even anger. They might make excuses for their child, ignore his or her mistakes or poor behavior, or accuse others of causing them (e.g., you, last year's teacher, a relative, or another student).

That's why it's important when talking to parents to be as positive as possible. Be sure to balance your concerns by pointing out their child's strengths and abilities. Talk about how these positive traits can help their child succeed in school. It also helps to be an active listener. Reflect back that you do hear and appreciate what parents are saying.

## Considerations for Students with IEPs

If your student does have an IEP, you might assume that the parents are aware and accepting of their child's disabilities and their impact on his or her behavior or academic performance. In many cases, this is a correct assumption. However, it's possible that your student's parents aren't completely aware of the full effect of their child's difficulties, these difficulties were never completely explained, or there have been recent changes. Or, if your student has received special education services for a long time, the parents may be frustrated with their child's slow progress or lingering needs. They might feel overwhelmed by their child's disabilities.

It will help as you talk to parents to emphasize the programs and support services that can help their child succeed academically. Talk about how parents can take advantage of these programs to make sure their child receives the best possible education. Help parents understand that together you are allies in their child's education.

## Communicating with "Hard-to-Reach" Parents

Parents need to feel welcome at school. For various reasons, your student's parents could feel uncomfortable in a school environment.

Some parents don't live within walking distance and have no transportation to get to school. Parents' work schedules might prevent them from being available during school hours.

Your school district could have parent participation programs that target "hard-to-reach" parents, or you may have to think of your own strategies. There are a number of effective, efficient, and practical ways you can correspond with your students' parents. Choose a system of communication that works for you. Consider the following:

**E-mail or voice mail.** Technology offers some great solutions for involving "hard-to-reach" parents in their child's education program. As more and more families join the "computer age," E-mail is fast replacing the phone call as the communication vehicle of choice. Also, many school districts have a voice-mail system so that parents can leave a message for you without pulling you away from class.

**Scheduled phone call.** For busy families, arranging a special time to call can make your communication attempts more efficient. For example, you could contact your student's parents at home every Wednesday at 5:30 p.m. or you could call during their lunch break at work on Fridays to report how the week went.

**Periodic meetings at school.** Perhaps your student's parents can drop by before school starts or at the end of the school day once a month for a brief 15- or 20-minute conference. Setting up a regular meeting time helps you and your student's parents remember the

meeting and schedule around it. For example, you could meet the first Friday of each month.

**Home-to-school logs.** A small notebook that goes back and forth between home and school can help keep you and your student's parents updated. This is particularly effective with small children or students who have severe needs. If your student works with a paraeducator or specialists, they can also use it to communicate with the parents regularly.

**Classroom parent visits.** Some parents can be persuaded to come to school if you ask them to share their expertise with the class. Contact parents at the beginning of the year about one thing they could do as a volunteer in the class for one day. Make their visit meaningful—work their presentation, hobby, talent, or skill into your lesson plan. For instance, an avid birdwatcher could help the science class develop a bird classification diagram or discuss the physics of flight. While at school, parents can observe their child's work, and you can give parents ideas on how to work with their child at home.

**Periodic home visits.** Meeting parents in their own home sends a strong message that you want them to be actively involved in their child's education. You may need to arrange with your principal for a substitute so that you're able to visit during school hours. If you can, go with another staff member, perhaps a specialist or a related services provider, such as a social worker. Try not to stay more than an hour. Make the visit meaningful. Write down insights your student's parents share with you. Ask to see your student's bedroom or study area; you may be able to make suggestions about the best way to organize the room for study time. For students with severe disabilities, you might take pictures of favorite belongings or parts of the house to use in your instruction at school.

**Classroom newsletter.** A newsletter that goes home with students or is posted on the school's Web site is a great way to let parents know what your students are studying. If your talents aren't in this area, you might recruit a couple of older or talented students or a few parents to write the newsletter based on information you give them. Put aside a space for "personalized" information so you can add notes pertaining to specific students before the newsletter goes home (e.g., in a column entitled "Just for Me" you could jot a message to Maria's parents remarking how glad you are that she is handing in all her homework).

**Progress reports.** Report cards and progress reports go home several times a year in most school districts. Some schools now have the ability to translate a child's report card in the parents' first language. IDEA required that parents of students with disabilities receive reports of their child's progress at least as often as parents of nondisabled students get progress reports. If your student has an IEP, you must inform his or her parents about progress toward the annual goals. In addition, you should tell parents whether their child's progress is sufficient to allow him or her to achieve IEP goals by the end of the year. If you aren't using the regular school report cards, you should use an effective reporting system. Unfortunately, some school districts require long written reports or multipaged reporting forms—a paperwork nightmare for teachers. If this is the case in your school, work with your administrators and parents to develop a simple format that parents can understand and teachers can complete efficiently.

### Communicating with "Hands-On" Parents

Some parents demand to be more involved in their student's education than you may feel is reasonable or wise. They may not trust that you'll adequately address their child's needs. With time, you can probably gain their trust and their demands will lessen. However, in the meantime, their primary request is frequent—even daily—communication. Normally, daily personal notes aren't feasible over an extended time period. Prepared checksheets can provide the same amount of information and take far less time. *(See Tool 6.1 on page 84: the Weekly Homework Log shows how Paula's teacher informed her parents about homework expectations.)*

School-home communication should not interfere with your teaching time. Try pointing out to your student's parents that the time you spend putting together information to send home could be better spent working with their child. If parents insist on a communication system that results in an unreasonable workload for you, and their child has an IEP, you can write in supplemental planning or conferencing time under "supports for personnel." Talk to your administrator or association representative if their demands continue; there may be school policies or contract language that could help you.

# Weekly Homework Log

Student: __Paula M.__                    Grade: __3rd__

Week of: _____          Teacher: __Ms. Tolliver__

| Subject | Monday | Tuesday | Wednesday | Thursday | Friday |
|---|---|---|---|---|---|
| **Reading** | Complete worksheets, pp. 5&6 | | Complete "Main Idea" worksheet | | Read chapter book for book report |
| **Spelling** | Study spelling list | Write down 10 words in sentences | | Study for Friday test | |
| **Writing** | | | Write 4-line poem using some spelling words | | Write book report for Monday |
| **Math** | | Problem-solving worksheet, p. 17 | | Record multiplication facts 1-5 on flashcards | |
| **Social Studies** | | Write down as many state capitals as you know | | Brainstorm 3 products most important to our state | |
| **Science** | Collect/Gather two types of rocks | | Complete Venn diagram on details of rocks | | |
| | | | | | |
| | | | | | |
| **Materials Needed** | Spelling list<br><br>Reading worksheets, pp. 5&6 | Spelling list<br><br>Math worksheet, p. 17 | Spelling list<br><br>Science worksheet<br><br>"Main Idea" worksheet | Spelling list<br><br>Index cards | Selected chapter book |

Parent Signature: _____          Date: _____

*Meeting the Challenge*

Think about using these common options, described below, to communicate with "hands-on" parents:

- E-mail and voice mail messages.

- Scheduled phone calls.

- Periodic meetings at school.

- Home-to-school logs.

- Classroom visits by parents.

- Periodic home visits.

- Classroom newsletter.

- Progress reports.

In addition, you can customize the following strategies to efficiently share information about your student's work:

**Parent volunteers.** Arrange for your student's parents to volunteer in the classroom—reading to individuals or small groups, assisting with learning centers, or working with students on the computer. While parents are busy working with other students, they can see first-hand how their child is doing.

**Monthly calendar of topics.** As you write your lesson plans for each month, you can fill in a one-page form that lists the major topics for the month, what pages to read in each text, key vocabulary, and related reading assignments. Copy this form and send it home to your student's parents so they can help their child at home.

**Study guides or curriculum review sheets.** Using study guides or review sheets for each theme or chapter of the text can help all your students. The guide or review should list key people or vocabulary, essential concepts, and any sequential procedures discussed in the chapter. Your students, especially those with special learning needs, can use the guide to focus on the "core," or most critical information, they must learn.

**School hotlines & web sites.** Many schools now have homework hotlines or Web sites teachers can use to tell parents what work needs to be done at home. You can use a special code that you share only with specific parents about the individual work their child is expected to complete when the work the entire class is doing is too difficult for that student. For example, if Tiffany is working on counting to 50 and answering personal information questions, but the entire class is studying the state capitals, your message might say: *I hope all my students can count to 50 and name where we live, because tonight's homework is to write sentences about each state, its capital, and one product important to the state's economy.* When Tiffany's parents call the hotline, they know that Tiffany's personal homework is anything you state you hope *all* your students can do. Therefore, for tonight's homework, Tiffany needs to count to 50 and state her address when asked, "Where do you live?"

**Annotated lesson plans for specific students.** Some of the team planning forms in Chapter 3 can be adapted to use as individualized lesson plans you can send home. This could be especially helpful if your student's program is significantly modified.

**Check-Off Sheets & Notes Home.** You can develop a standard "Home Report" that includes the day's typical schedule or activities in a check-off format. A couple of sections could be left "open" for comments or to report on special events. These can be particularly effective to use as daily reports on your student's behavior. *(See Tool 6.2, the Daily Home Report, on page 88.)*

# Parent-Teacher Conferences

Parent-teacher conferences are held at least once a year in nearly every school district in the country. While they're an excellent way for parents and teachers to communicate with one another, they are typically one of the most stressful events of the year—for teachers and parents alike. When students are struggling academically, or they have behavior problems or disabilities that affect their learning, meeting with their parents can create unanticipated tensions.

Here are some suggestions for how to prepare for your parent-teacher conferences and how to make them productive for everyone involved:

### Before the Conference

- Send home personal letters to notify parents of conference dates. Ask parents to RSVP by a specific date. Then send reminders—E-mail or phone "hard-to-reach" parents a couple days before the conference date.

- Send home an agenda for the meeting that includes time for parents to ask questions. Emphasize how important it is for them to attend.

- Coordinate conference times with specialists, special area teachers, or support staff who might be involved with students' programs.

- Try to schedule the length of the conferences based on the needs of your students. You could block out two consecutive periods if you suspect certain parents will need more time.

- Send home a planning sheet to help parents prepare for the meeting. *(See Tool 6.3, the Conference Planning Sheet, on page 89.)* Suggest parents complete the planning sheet and bring it with them to the conference.

### Prepare for the Conference

- Prepare a folder with samples of your students' work. Update your grade book and make sure you have accounted for all projects and homework assignments. If you plan to talk about problems students are having in class, include work samples that illustrate these difficulties in the folders.

- If appropriate, put together folders for parents with suggested activities or study strategies they can use at home.

- Think about what you plan to say. Write down questions you want to ask.

## Set the Stage

- Make the conference area comfortable for both you and your student's parents. Put out cookies and bottles of water for parents in a designated "waiting area."

- In the waiting area, put out flyers about parenting, after-school activities in your area, a copy of your classroom rules and procedures, brief descriptions of your curriculum, a syllabus, or grade-level expectations.

- Provide suggestions about how parents can make the conference productive. Put out extra copies of the *Conference Planning Sheet* so parents can complete it while they wait.

- Set up a comfortable, private area for the conference with adult-sized chairs, if you have them. A round table with plenty of space to look at students' work is preferable. Include some blank paper and pencils or pens for parents to take notes.

## During the Conference

- Dress professionally and start the conference on time.

- Welcome parents at the door. Shake their hands and introduce yourself. Thank them for coming to meet with you.

- Share something positive about their child and ask parents about their child's participation in a home or community activity (e.g., sports, music lessons, visits to grandparents).

- Talk about students' strengths first.

- Discuss students' progress and show examples of their work.

- Share any concerns you have directly and calmly.

- Ask parents to comment on their child's study habits at home or their perspectives of his or her class work.

- Ask parents for their support. Discuss one or two specific ways they can help at home. Provide a list of suggestions, if appropriate.

- Make plans for how you will communicate with parents and how, together, you and they will monitor students' progress.

- Summarize the major points of the conference and end on a positive note.

- Walk parents to the door and thank them for coming.

- Make a few notes about the highlights of the conference, especially any actions you agreed to take.

# Daily Home Report

**Student:** Carl H.　　　　　　　　**Grade:** Kindergarten

**Date:** _____　　**Teacher:** Ms. Kinzer

**I am working on:** (goal)　Identifying five letters of the alphabet.

**Today, I:**

|  | not at all | sometimes | most of the time |
|---|:---:|:---:|:---:|
| Followed directions | 1 | 2 | ③ |
| Completed my work in class | 1 | 2 | ③ |
| Followed classroom rules | 1 | ② | 3 |
| Kept my work space neat | ① | 2 | 3 |
| Got along well with others | 1 | 2 | ③ |

**Teacher's Comments:**　Carl identified four out of five letters today! I had to remind him three

times to clean up his work space. Maybe he can practice by helping you clean up after dinner tonight.

Signature:　*Ms. Kinzer*

**Parent's Comments:**_____

_____

_____

Signature: _____

# Conference Planning Sheet for Parents

A conference with your child's teacher is scheduled for _____ at _____ in room _____. This planning sheet will help you think about what you may want to discuss during the conference. Please bring it to the conference with you.

1) **Talk to your child before the conference.** Explain that you are going to be meeting with his or her teacher. Tell your child you want to help the teacher as much as you can. Find out what his or her best subjects are and which subjects he or she likes the least. Ask why certain subjects are easier than others. Also, ask your child if there is anything you should talk about with his or her teacher(s).
   - What questions or concerns does your child have about school? (Complete this section with your child.)

2) **To help you prepare, think about the following questions before you come to the conference.**
   - What are my goals for my child this year?
   - Is my child dealing with any health problems or family situations that could affect his or her behavior or academic progress?
   - What do I want the teacher to know about my child. (for example, personality, habits, hobbies)?

3) **To use the conference time efficiently, write down any questions you have for your child's teacher(s) about the curriculum or classroom expectations.**
   For example:
   - What skills and knowledge is my child expected to master this year?
   - How will my child be evaluated? What kinds of tests will he or she take?
   - How well does my child get along with others?
   - Is my child working up to his or her ability?
   - Has my child missed any classes? Does he or she hand in homework on time?
   - Does my child participate in class discussions?
   - What type of special help is available to help my child progress?
   - Other questions: _____

4) **Children do better in school when their parents are actively involved in their education. Before you leave the conference, ask this question:**
   - How can I help my child do better in school?

## KEY POINTS

Parents are an essential part of your student's "team." You can communicate positively with them by:

1. Letting parents know how and when to contact you.

2. Speaking with parents directly, truthfully, and clearly about your concerns.

3. Using active listening techniques.

4. Making an effort to understand parents' perspective.

5. Communicating with parents frequently through a variety of efficient and effective methods.

# Glossary

**504 Accommodation Plans** – Plans written under the provisions of Section 504 of the Rehabilitation Act of 1973 that outline the types of accommodations needed by a student who is disabled.

**Accommodations** – Changes in the environment, materials, presentation, or response mode to allow a student access to instruction and an opportunity to participate in learning.

**Alternative strategies** – Various teaching techniques and strategies developed and used to meet students' individual needs.

**Annual Goals** – Estimated learning outcomes within an academic year.

**Baseline Data** – A starting point from which to monitor changes or improvement in student performance.

**Benchmarks** – Intermediate milestones that must be attained at specified time periods as student progresses toward achieving an annual goal.

**Classroom-Based Assessments (CBAs)** – Assessments conducted in the classroom or by classroom staff based on curriculum expectations, such as quizzes, mid-term exams, or reading tests.

**Effective Instruction** – Instruction that responds to students' needs while building on their strengths.

**Functional Behavioral Assessment (FBA)** – Specific steps used to observe and identify problematic student behaviors.

**Inclusion** – While not defined in law, this term refers to the practice of educating students with disabilities full time in the general education environment.

**Individualized Education Program (IEP)** – A written statement or plan for a specific child with a disability that is developed, reviewed, and revised at an IEP meeting. The IEP guides the delivery of special education supports and services for that child.

**Individuals with Disabilities Education Act of 1997 (IDEA '97)** – The federal law that stipulates how school districts must identify children with disabilities and provide them with special education and related services.

**Instructional Reading Level** – The level a student can read given assistance from the teacher, with 90–95 percent accuracy.

**Interim Alternative Educational Setting** – A separate or different educational program or school setting that meets the student's need to continue to progress in the general curriculum and to receive those services and modifications described in his or her IEP.

**Learning Style** – A description of how a student learns best, usually referring to which modality, sensory channel, or learning strategy is strongest (e.g., auditory vs. visual; linguistic vs. kinesthetic)

**Least Restrictive Environment** – A requirement defined in IDEA '97 that, to the maximum extent appropriate, children with disabilities must be educated with children who do not have disabilities. The law also states that special classes, separate schools, or other removal of children with disabilities from the general education environment may occur only if the nature or severity of the child's disability is such that education in general classes with the use of supplementary aids and services cannot be achieved satisfactorily.

**Modifications** – Changes in curriculum content, type of instruction, or materials that are likely to alter student expectations or learning outcome.

**Observation-Based Assessments (OBAs)** – An evaluation of a student's behavior based on observations made in the classroom environment.

**Performance Criteria** – The expected level of performance for a learning outcome written in measurable terms.

**Present Levels of Performance** – How a student is currently performing in meeting school and classroom expectations. It includes classroom-based assessments, the multidisciplinary team evaluation results, and observations by teachers, parents, related service providers, paraeducators, administrators, and others. For preschool children, it addresses how the child participates in appropriate activities normally expected at his or her age.

**Related Services** – Services a student needs in order to benefit from special education. Specific services listed in IDEA '97 as "related services" include: audiology, counseling, early identification and assessment, medical, occupational therapy, orientation and mobility, parent counseling and training, physical therapy, psychological, recreation, rehabilitation counseling, school health, social work services in the schools, speech-language pathology, and transportation. States may define additional related services.

**Short-Term Objectives** – Intermediate steps representing discrete skills that must be learned as a student progresses toward achieving an annual goal.

**Special Education** – Specially designed instruction for students with special needs.

**Transition Services** – A coordinated set of activities that prepare students with disabilities for adult life, including developing postsecondary education and career goals, getting work experience while still in school, and linking with adult services such as the vocational rehabilitation agency.

# References

## Chapter 1:

Snow, Catherine E., Susan M. Burns, and Peg Griffin, eds. *Preventing Reading Difficulties in Young Children.* Committee on the Prevention of Reading Difficulties in Young Children. Washington, D.C.: National Academy Press. 1998.

Clay, Marie M. *An Observation Survey of Early Literacy Achievement.* Portsmouth, N.H.: Heinemann Education. 1998.

McTighe, Jay and Steven Ferrara. *Assessing Learning in the Classroom.* Washington, D.C.: National Education Association. 1998.

Holcomb, Sabrina, Ed Amundson, and Patti Ralabate. *The New IDEA Survival Guide.* Washington, D.C.: NEA Professional Library. 2000.

## Chapter 2:

*Applying Positive Behavioral Supports and Functional Behavioral Assessment in Schools.* Washington, D.C.: OSEP Center on Positive Behavioral Interventions and Support, US Department of Education. 1999.

Canter, Lee and Marlene Canter. *Assertive Discipline.* Los Angeles, Calif.: Canter and Associates. 1982.

*Educational Strategies for Children with Emotional and Behavioral Problems.* Washington, D.C.: Center for Effective Collaboration and Practice, American Institutes for Research. 2000.

Sugai, George and Robert Horner. "School Climate and Discipline: Going to Scale, a Framing Paper for the National Summit on Shared Implementation on IDEA." June 2001. Center on Positive Behavioral Interventions and Supports, University of Oregon.

Silverstein, Robert. *An Overview of the Disability Policy Framework: A Guidepost for Analyzing Public Policy.* Washington, D.C.: Center for the Study and Advancement of Disability Policy. 2000.

## Chapter 3:

Benninghof, Anne M. *Ideas for Inclusion, The Classroom Teacher's Guide to Integrating Students with Severe Disabilities.* Longmont, Colo.: Sopris West. 1993.

McLaughlin, Margaret. *Appropriate Inclusion and Paraprofessionals: Changing Roles and Expectations.* Washington, D.C.: National Education Association.

*The NEA Paraeducator Handbook.* Washington, D.C.: National Education Association. 2000.

*Paraeducators and IDEA: What Paraeducators Need To Know To Advocate for Themselves.* Washington, D.C.: National Education Association. 2000.

Vaughn, Sharon, Jeanne Shay-Schumm, and Maria Elena Arguelles. "The ABCDEs of Co-Teaching." *Teaching Exceptional Children.* Vol. 30, No. 2, November/December 1997.

**Chapter 4:**

"Dressing Your IEPs for the General Education Climate." *Remedial and Special Education.* Vol. 15, No. 5. September 1994. Austin, Tex.: Pro-Ed.

*A Guide to the Individualized Education Program.* Washington, D.C.: Office of Special Education and Rehabilitative Services, U.S. Department of Education. 2000.

*IEP Team Guide.* Arlington, Va.: Council for Exceptional Children. 1999.

Marzano, Robert J. and John S. Kendall. *Implementing Standards-Based Education.* Washington, D.C.: National Education Association. 1998.

Lignugaris-Kraft, Benjamin, Nancy Marchand-Martella, and Ronald C. Martella. "Writing Better Goals and Short-Term Objectives or Benchmarks." *Teaching Exceptional Children.* Vol. 34, No. 1. September-October 2001. Council for Exceptional Children.

**Chapter 5:**

Benninghof, Anne. *SenseAble Strategies: Including Diverse Learners Through Multisensory Strategies.* Longmont, Colo.: Sopris West. 1998.

Haigh, John. "Accommodations, Modifications, and Alternates for Instruction and Assessment, Maryland/Kentucky Report 5." December 1999. National Center on Educational Outcomes.

*Making Assessment Accommodations: A Toolkit for Educators.* Arlington, Va.: Council for Exceptional Children. 2000. (Video)

**Chapter 6:**

*Best of Teacher-to-Teacher: The Ultimate Beginner's Guide.* (NEA's Teacher-to-Teacher Series). Washington, D.C.: NEA Professional Library. 2000.

Brooks-Bonner, Lorna. "Responding to Aggressive Parents." *School Safety.* Spring, 1993. Westlake Village, Calif.: National School Safety Center.

Canter, Lee and Marlene Canter. 1988. *Assertive Discipline for Parents.* New York, N.Y.: Harper & Row.

Epstein, Joyce L. "School/Family/Community Partnerships, Caring for the Children We Share." *Phi Delta Kappa.* May 1995, pp. 701-72.

*Parent Conference Book.* Santa Monica, Calif.: Lee Canter & Associates. 1989.

Swick, Kevin J. "Teacher-Parent Partnerships." *ERIC Digest,* ED351149.

Wilmes, David and David J. *Parenting for Prevention: How To Raise a Child To Say No to Alcohol/Drugs.* Minneapolis, Minn.: Johnson Institute Books. 1988.

# Resources

## Books

Algozzine, Bob and Pam Kay, eds. *Preventing Problem Behaviors.* Thousand Oaks, Calif.: Corwin Press, Inc. 2002.
A handbook that discusses successful prevention methods for behavior problems, such as school-wide discipline policies, development of social skills, and improving overall behavior skills.

Cohen, Mary Kemper, et al. *Survival Guide for the First-Year Special Education Teacher.* Arlington, Va.: Council for Exceptional Children. 1994.
This book offers preparation tips, hints for establishing good rapport, and ways to manage stress for all teachers new to the profession.

Emanuel, Ellen J. and David R. Johnson. *Issues Influencing the Future of Transition Programs and Services in the United States.* Minneapolis/St. Paul, Minn.: Institute on Community Integration at the University of Minnesota. 2000.
This collection of articles comes from leading researchers in the field of secondary special education and transitional services for students with disabilities. Among the many topics discussed are activities that satisfy the components of IDEA, parent and student collaboration on the learning process, and the importance of teacher attitudes.

Hemmeter, Mary Louise, et al. *DEC Recommended Practices: Improving Practices for Young Children with Special Needs and Their Families.* Thousand Oaks, Calif.: Sopris West. 2001.
The Division of Early Childhood (DEC) is a branch of the Council for Exceptional Children that focuses on children from birth to age eight. This book includes appropriate educational practices, case studies, assessment activities, and hints for planning.

Hilton, Alan and Ravic Ringlaben, eds. *Best and Promising Practices in Developmental Disabilities.* Austin, Tex.: Pro-Ed. 1998.
This book outlines the various stages and steps involved in teaching students with disabilities. Among those described are definition and placement, assessment and curriculum, specific instructional strategies, individual needs, and the importance of family and community involvement.

Jakubecy, Jennifer J. and James M. Kauffman, eds. *Assessment for Effective Intervention, Special Issue: EBD Assessment.* Austin, Tex.: Journal of the Council for Educational Diagnostic Services. 2000.
This book helps professionals assess individuals with disabilities and/or who are gifted under a broad framework, rather than just through standardized testing.

Kame'enui, Edward J., and Deborah C. Simmons. *Toward Successful Inclusion of Students with Disabilities: The Architecture of Instruction.* Thousand Oaks, Calif.: The Council for Exceptional Children. 1999.
An outgrowth of an ERIC/OSEP Special Project, this book details a number of pressing issues regarding children with mental and physical disabilities, including

cognitive processing of information, designing and accessing curriculum, and six principles of effective curriculum design.

Kohler, Dr. Paula D. and Lisa K. Hood. *Improving Student Outcomes: Promising Practices and Programs for 1999-2000.* Urbana-Champaign, Ill.: Board of Trustees of University of Illinois. 1999. This is directory of innovative approaches for providing transition services for students with disabilities.

McLaughlin, Margaret J. and Victor Nolet. *Accessing the General Curriculum: Including Students with Disabilities in Standards-Based Reform.* Thousand Oaks, Calif.: Corwin Press, Inc. 2000. This handbook explains IDEA requirements and their relationship to standards-based reform. It addresses various types of curriculum, how to evaluate teaching effectiveness, and how to develop IEPs that best serve students with disabilities and special needs.

Pickett, Anna Lou and Kent Gerlach. *Supervising Paraeducators in School Settings.* Arlington, Va.: Council for Exceptional Children. 1997. This is the first book written about issues associated specifically with managing and supervising paraeducators, such as team roles, professional and ethical responsibilities and obligations, and administrative issues.

Siegal, Lawrence M. *The Complete IEP Guide: How To Advocate for Your Special Ed Child* (2nd edition). Berkeley, Calif.: Nolo. 2001. Written from an attorney's perspective, this book is a reader-friendly description of special education laws and policy.

Sitlington, Patricia L., et al. *Access for Success Handbook on Transition Assessment.* Arlington, Va.: Council for Exceptional Children. 1996. What is a transition and how can we make assessments on it? How can a transition be used for IEP planning? Who are the key players in the transition process? This book answers all of these questions and many related ones, as well.

Thurlow, M.L., et al. *Testing Students with Disabilities: Practical Strategies for Complying with District and State Requirements.* Thousand Oaks, Calif.: Corwin Press. 1998. This guide helps explain issues pertaining to testing of students with disabilities. It gives educators a grasp of the issues and helps them implement meaningful tests for students in general.

## CD-ROMs

Council for Exceptional Children. *Discover IDEA CD 2000.* Arlington, Va.: Council for Exceptional Children. 2000. The 2000 edition of this resource contains updates from the U.S. Department of Education on a number of critical issues, in addition to the Headstart Disability Regulations. This CD-ROM has a user-friendly version of the IDEA regulations, as well as over 50 policy and practices publications that answer viewers' questions and point them in the right direction on the Internet.

Families and Advocates Partnerships for Education. *Positive Behavioral Interventions: Parents Need to Know.* Minneapolis: Pacer Center. 1999.
Information for parents about positive behavioral strategies is explained on this CD.

*The IEP Planner-Transition Skills.* Mac or Windows. Rodan Associates. 2001.
This CD demonstrates how to develop an IEP with a focus on transition planning.

# Video

Bateman, Barbara D. *Understanding IDEA 1997 and the 1999 Regulations.* Arlington, Va.: Council For Exceptional Children. 1999.
This tape tackles IDEA changes in areas such as discipline, legal procedures, and team membership.

Council for Exceptional Children. *Focus on the IEP and Performance Assessment.* Arlington, Va.: Council for Exceptional Children. 1998.
In this video, experts give their views on student involvement, performance assessment, benchmarks, short-term objectives, accommodations, alternative assessments, and involving the general education teacher.

*IDEA Reauthorization Discipline and Creating Positive Learning Environments.* Arlington, Va.: Council for Exceptional Children. 1998.
This video answers questions about IDEA requirements related to behavioral intervention plans, the role of the IEP team, Interim Alternative Education Settings (IAES), and suspension and expulsion. It also discusses positive supports, developing safe schools, and cultural variations related to behavior.

Friend, Marilyn and Lynne Cook. *The Power of Two: Making a Difference Through Co-Teaching.* Elephant Rock Productions. 1996.
The focus of this video is how to effectively engage in co-teaching.

Hanlon, Grace M. *A New IDEA for Special Education: Understanding the System and the New Law.* Arlington, Va.: Council for Exceptional Children. 1998.
This tape promotes the importance of collaboration among general educators, special educators, and parents by introducing the requirements of IDEA '97 to all parties. It also highlights the referral process, evaluation, IEPs, placement and other services, preparation for transitions, discipline, mediation, and standardized testing requirements.

# Web Resources

## Special Education Issues and Practices

**ERIC Clearinghouse on Elementary and Early Childhood Education**

University of Illinois at Urbana-Champaign

Children's Research Center

51 Gerty Drive

Urbana, IL 61820-7469

Phone: 217-333-1386

Toll free: 800-583-4135

Fax: 217-333-3767

E-mail: ericeece@uiuc.edu

Web: http://ericeece.org/

Web: http://npin.org (National Parent Information Network)

**ERIC Clearinghouse for Special and Gifted Education**

The Council for Exceptional Children

1110 North Glebe Road, Suite 300

Arlington, VA 22201-5704

Phone/TTY: (800) 328-0272

Fax: (703) 620-2521

Email: ericec@cec.sped.org

Web: http://ericec.org

**http://www.ideapractices.org**

Web site for ASPIIRE IDEA Partnership—a coalition of associations representing general and special education personnel who service students with disabilities.

**http://www.cec.sped.org**

Web site for the Council for Exceptional Children—an organization that focuses on the education of students with disabilities.

**http://www.ideainfo.org**

Web site for IDEA Partnerships, four national projects funded by the U.S. Department of Education's Office of Special Education and Rehabilitative Services (Office of Special Education Programs) to deliver a common message about IDEA '97.

**http://www.ed.gov/offices/OSERS/**

U.S. Department of Education's Office of Special Education and Rehabilitative Services.

**http://nichcy.org**

National Information Center for Children and Youth with Disabilities (NICHCY).

## Assessment:

**http://www.coled.umn.edu/nceo**

Web site for the National Center for Educational Outcomes, a national project concerned with accountability and assessments of all students, including students with disabilities.

## Accommodations and Modifications

**http://www.cast.org**

Web site for the Center for Applied Special Technology, an educational, not-for-profit organization that uses technology to expand opportunities for all people, including those with disabilities.

**http://www.nde.state.ne.us/SPED**

Web site for the Nebraska Department of Education, which includes examples of classroom accommodations.

**http://www.palaestra.com**

Web site and online forum regarding adaptive physical education for students with disabilities.

**http://www.ldonline.org**

Online guide for parents and teachers regarding learning disabilities.

**http://www.resa.net/assistive/**

Web site for the Wayne County Regional Educational Service Agency in Michigan, regarding accommodations and assistive technology.

## Parent Communications

**Alliance for Parental Involvement in Education**

29 Kinderhook Street

Chatham, NY 12037

Phone: 518-392-6900

E-mail: allpie@taconic.net

Web: http://www.croton.com/allpie/

**The National PTA**

330 Wabash Avenue, Suite 2100

Chicago, IL 60611

Phone: 312-670-6782

E-mail: info@pta.org

Web: http://www.pta.org

**The Families and Advocates Partnership for Education (FAPE)**

PACER Center

4826 Chicago Avenue South

Minneapolis, MN 55417-1098

Toll-free: (888) 248-0822

Phone: (612) 827-2966

Fax: (612) 827-3065

Email: fape@pacer.org

Web: http://www.fape.org

# Appendix Toolkit

In this appendix, you will find blank copies of the Toolkit resources discussed throughout the book. Also included are several additional resources that were not discussed in the body of the book but are made available for your use: a) San Diego Quick Assessment for determining students' reading levels; b) Revised Dolch List for assessing sight word vocabulary skills; c) Emergent Literary Checklist for evaluating early reading and pre-reading skills; d) Curriculum-Based Assessment: Fluency and Accuracy for testing reading fluency skills; e) Developmental Reading Scale for assessing reading skills using a holistic developmental rubric; f) Reading Comprehension Rubric for judging reading comprehension skills using a holistic rubric; g) Intervention Strategies Menu for reporting which intervention strategies were used in the classroom; and h) Special Area Class Communication Form for informing special area teachers of your student's performance levels and participation skills.

## Assessments

San Diego Quick Assessment

Revised Dolch List

Simplified Emergent Literacy Checklist

Curriculum-Based Reading Assessment: Fluency & Accuracy

Developmental Reading Scale

Reading Comprehension Rubric

Analytic Rubric of Prewriting Skills

Checklist for Expository Written Language Skills

Holistic Rubric of Expository Written Language

Intervention Progress Sheet

Intervention Strategies Menu

## Behavior-Based Assessments

Observable Positive and Negative Behaviors Chart

Behavior Observation Form

Behavior Observation Tally Sheet

Behavior Intervention Plan

Possible Data Collection Methods

## Collaborative Teams

Sequence-of-the-Day Planning Sheet

Team Teaching/Co-Teaching Daily Lesson Plan

Special Area Class Communication Form

## Individualized Education Plans

Sample Format for Writing Goals, Objectives, and Benchmarks

100 Active Verbs for Writing Goals, Objectives, and Benchmarks

## Accommodations and Modifications

Accommodations and Modifications Planning Worksheet

Accommodations and Modifications Checklist

Accommodations and Modifications Assessment Checklist

## Parent Communication

Conference Planning Sheet for Parents

Weekly Homework Log

Daily Home Report

# San Diego Quick Assessment

Student: _____ Grade: _____

Date: _____ Instructional Level: _____

| Preprimer Level | Primer | First |
|---|---|---|
| see | you | road |
| play | come | live |
| me | not | thank |
| at | with | when |
| run | jump | bigger |
| go | help | how |
| and | is | always |
| look | work | night |
| can | are | spring |
| here | this | today |

| Second | Third | Fourth |
|---|---|---|
| our | city | decided |
| please | middle | served |
| myself | moment | amazed |
| town | frightened | silent |
| early | exclaimed | wrecked |
| send | several | improved |
| wide | lonely | certainly |
| believe | drew | entered |
| quietly | since | realized |
| carefully | straight | interrupted |

Scoring Key: Two words wrong is Instructional Level; One word wrong is Independent Level.

From LaPray, M.H., and Ross, R.R. (1969, January). The graded word list: Quick guage of reading ability. *Journal of Reading, 12*, 305-307. Reprinted with permission of the International Reading Association. All rights reserved.

# Revised Dolch List

Student: _____ Grade: _____

Date: _____ Teacher: _____

| | | | | | |
|---|---|---|---|---|---|
| a* | could | he* | might | same | told |
| about* | cut | heard | more | saw | too |
| across | did | help | most | say | took |
| after | didn't | her* | much | see | toward |
| again | do | here | must | she* | try |
| all* | does | high | my | short | turn |
| always | done | him | near | should | two |
| am | don't | his* | need | show | under |
| an* | down | hold | never | six | up* |
| and* | draw | hot | next | small | upon |
| another | eat | how | new | so* | us |
| any | enough | I* | no | some* | use |
| are* | even | I'm | not* | soon | very |
| around | every | if* | now | start | walk |
| as* | far | in* | of* | still | want |
| ask | fast | into | off | stop | warm |
| at* | find | is* | oh | take | was* |
| away | first | it* | old | tell | we* |
| be* | five | its | on* | ten | well |
| because | for* | just | once | than | went |
| been | found | keep | one* | that* | were* |
| before | four | kind | only | the* | what* |
| began | from* | know | open | their* | when* |
| best | full | last | or* | them | where |
| better | gave | leave | other | then | which |
| big | get | left | our | there* | while |
| black | give | let | out* | these | white |
| blue | go | light | over | they* | who |
| both | going | like | own | think | why |
| bring | gone | little | play | this* | will |
| but* | good | long | put | those | with* |
| by* | got | look | ran | thought | work |
| call | green | made | read | three | would* |
| came | grow | make | red | through | yes |
| can* | had* | many | right | to* | yet |
| close | hard | may | round | today | you* |
| cold | has | me | run | together | your |
| come | have* | mean | said* | | |

*one of the 50 most common words.

The rationale and research for this list is described in Johns, J.L. (1981). The development of the revised Dolch list. *Illinois School Research and Development, 17,* 15–24. From Jerry L. Johns, Susan Davis Lenski, and Laurie Elish-Piper, *Teaching Beginning Readers: Linking Assessment and Instruction (2nd ed.).* Copyright© 2002 by Kendall/Hunt Publishing Company.

# Simplified Emergent Literacy Checklist

Student: _____ Grade: _____

Date: _____ Teacher: _____

**Directions:** Give the child a picture book with print and ask him/her to read it to you. Observe his/her attention to the pictures and speaking behavior then look at the descriptions below. Use these descriptions to determine the child's level of emergent literacy.

| Broad Categories | Brief Explanation of Categories |
|---|---|
| **Level 1**<br><br>Attending to Pictures<br><br>Not Forming Stories | ■ The child is "reading" by looking at the storybook's pictures.<br>■ The child's speech is just about the picture in view.<br>■ The child is not "weaving a story" across the pages. |
| **Level 2**<br><br>Attending to Pictures<br><br>Forming Oral Stories | ■ The child is "reading" by looking at the storybook's pictures.<br>■ The child's speech weaves a story across the pages.<br>■ The wording and the intonation are like that of someone telling a story:<br>　■ Like a conversation about the pictures, or<br>　■ Like a fully recited story, in which the listener can see the pictures (and often must see them to understand the child's story). |
| **Level 3**<br><br>Attending to Pictures<br><br>Mixed Reading and Storytelling | ■ The child is "reading" by looking at the storybook's pictures.<br>■ The child's speech fluctuates between sounding like a story-teller with oral intonation and sounding like a reader, with reading intonation.<br>■ To fit this category, the majority of the reading attempt must show fluctuations between storytelling and reading. |
| **Level 4**<br><br>Attending to Pictures<br><br>Forming Written Stories | ■ The child is "reading" by looking at the storybook's pictures.<br>■ The child's speech sounds as if the child is reading, both in wording and intonation.<br>■ The listener rarely needs to look at the pictures in order to understand the story.<br>■ If the listener closes his/her eyes, he or she would generally think the child is reading from print. |
| **Level 5**<br><br>Attending to Print | ■ The child is attending to print as the source of the reading in one of these subcategories:<br>　■ Refusing to read based on print awareness<br>　■ Reading aspectually (focused on comprehension of print) with emphasis on words and/or letter-sound relationships and/or comprehension<br>　■ Reading with strategies imbalanced<br>　■ Reading independently (conventional reading). |

Reprinted with permission by the International Reading Association and the author from: Sulzby, Elizabeth. *Children's Emergent Reading of Favorite Storybooks: A Developmental Study.* Reading Research Quarterly; volume 20, number 4, pages 458-481; 1985

# Curriculum Based Reading Assessment: Fluency and Accuracy

Student:_____  Grade: _____

Date: _____  Instructional Level: _____

Teacher: _____  Independent Level: _____

## Grade Level Reading Fluency Standards

### Grade level of text

| WRC | 1 | 2 | 3 | 4 | 5 | 6 |
|-----|---|---|---|---|---|---|
| 180 | | | | | | |
| 170 | | | | | | |
| 160 | | | | | | |
| 150 | | | | | | |
| 140 | | | | | | |
| 130 | | | | | | |
| 120 | | | | | | |
| 110 | | | | | | |
| 100 | | | | | | |
| 90 | | | | | | |
| 80 | | | | | | |
| 70 | | | | | | |
| 60 | | | | | | |
| 50 | | | | | | |
| 40 | | | | | | |
| 30 | | | | | | |
| 20 | | | | | | |
| 10 | | | | | | |
| 0 | | | | | | |

**Fluency Levels and Standards**

**Grade**

| | |
|---|---|
| 1.1 | 35/40 seg. PS |
| 1.2 | 35/40 NW |
| 1.3 | 40/60 WRC |
| 2.1 | 50/70 WRC |
| 2.2 | 70/90 WRC |
| 2.3 | 90/110 WRC |
| 3.1 | 80/100 WRC |
| 3.2 | 90/120 WRC |
| 3.3 | 120/140 WRC |
| 4.1 | 100/120 WRC |
| 4.2 | 115/130 WRC |
| 4.3 | 120/140 WRC |
| 5.1 | 110/130 WRC |
| 5.2 | 120/140 WRC |
| 5.3 | 140/160 WRC |
| 6 & up | 150+ WRC |

CBA should be done 3x per year:

1.1 = fall
1.2 = winter
1.3 = spring

Standards based on suggestions of Hasbrouck and Tindal, 1992

WRC = Words read correctly, i.e. total read in one minute less the errors

NW = Nonsense words

PS = Phonemes segmented (breaks words into syllables)

Each score represents the mean score of 3 reading probes, WRC (for grade 1.1 set = phonemes segmented and for 1.2 NW = nonsense words read)

Hasbrouck, Jan E., & Tintal, Gerald, (1992). Curriculum-Based Oral Reading Fluency Norms for Students in Grades 2 through 5. *Teaching Exceptional Children, 24* (3), 41-44.

# Developmental Reading Scale

**Student:**_____ **Grade:** _____

**Date:** _____ **Developmental Reading Level:**_____

### Emergent Reader

☐ follows along in the text when adult reads

☐ is aware of relationship of printed text to oral language

☐ uses picture cues when recalling story

☐ pretends to read; memorizes favorite stories

### Beginner Reader

☐ reads work-for-word; struggles with unfamiliar material

☐ has limited sight vocabulary of one- and two-syllable words

☐ attempts to pronounce and figure out meaning of new words

☐ demonstrates comprehension of simple text

☐ occasionally monitors comprehension and self-corrects

### Competent Reader

☐ reads familiar material comfortably

☐ has large sight vocabulary

☐ uses context clues to figure out meaning of unfamiliar words

☐ actively constructs meaning

☐ regularly monitors comprehension and self-corrects

### Fluent Reader

☐ reads fluently with expression; has extensive sight vocabulary

☐ readily determines meaning of unfamiliar words using context clues

☐ reads a wide variety of materials with understanding

☐ independently monitors comprehension; appropriately applies comprehension strategies

From *Assessing Learning in the Classroom* by Jay McTighe and Steven Ferrara. National Education Association

# Reading Comprehension Rubric

**Student:** _____ **Grade:** _____

**Date:** _____ **Reading Comprehension Level:** _____

| Rating Scale | Evaluative Criteria |
|:---:|:---|
| 4 | Reader displays a sophisticated understanding of the text with substantial evidence of constructing meaning. Multiple connections are made between the text and the reader's ideas/experiences. Interpretations are sophisticated and directly supported by appropriate text references. Reader explicitly takes a critical stance (e.g., analyzes the author's style, questions the text, provides alternate interpretations, views the text from multiple perspectives). |
| 3 | Reader displays a solid understanding of the text with clear evidence of constructing meaning. Connections are made between the text and the reader's ideas/experiences. Interpretations are made and generally supported by appropriate text references. Reader may reveal a critical stance toward the text. |
| 2 | Reader displays a partial understanding of the text with some evidence of constructing meaning. A connection may be made between the text and the reader's ideas/experiences, but it is not developed. Interpretations are not made and/or not supported by appropriate text references. Reader shows no evidence of a critical stance toward the text. |
| 1 | Reader displays a superficial understanding of the text with limited evidence of constructing meaning. No connections are made between the text and the reader's ideas/experiences. Reader provides no interpretations or evidence of a critical stance. |
| 0 | Reader displays no evidence of text comprehension or constructive meaning. |

From *Assessing Learning in the Classroom* by Jay McTighe and Steven Ferrara. National Education Association

# Analytic Rubric of Prewriting Skills

**Student:** _____    **Grade:** _____

**Date:** _____    **Teacher:** _____

## Task:

Now that you've finished your writing assignment, take a look at the chart below and find which prewriting skill you used.

|  | **Novice** | **Developing** | **Expected** | **Mastery** |
|---|---|---|---|---|
| **Idea Generation** | I thought of one idea and started writing. | I thought of a few ideas and then chose one. | I thought of many ideas and then chose one. | I thought of several ideas, solicited ideas from others, and then chose one. |
| **Organization of Ideas** | I began writing without a plan. | I jotted a few notes but did not use a graphic organizer. | I used a graphic organizer to develop a detailed plan. | I used a detailed graphic organizer that included my ideas as well as suggestions from others. |
| **Consideration of Audience and Purpose** | I did not identify an audience or a purpose. | I identified an audience and purpose but did not write with them in mind. | I wrote with my audience and purpose in mind. | I gathered additional information about my audience and/or purpose before I began writing. |
| **Writing Form and Format** | I selected neither the appropriate form nor format. | I selected either the appropriate form or format. | I selected both the appropriate form and format. | After considering possible alternatives, I selected the most appropriate form and format. |

Developed by Lori Windler, East Tipp Middle School, Lafayette, IN March 2002

# Checklist for Expository Written Language Skills

**Student:** _____ **Grade:** _____

**Date:** _____ **Teacher:** _____

## *Procedure:*

Under each trait listed below, check all that apply to your student's writing. Add the total number of items checked and enter the total on the line at the bottom. If all the descriptors under each trait are present, the total score is 24.

**Focus**
___ topic is clearly addressed/established
___ topic is carefully introduced at the beginning with at least 3 support statements
___ topic remains clear throughout

**Development**
___ focus is on topic without irrelevant information
___ ideas are fully developed
___ ideas/theme is unique/creative
___ sustains reader interest

**Organization**
___ ideas are sequenced
___ includes clear beginning, middle, and end
___ uses a summary statement
___ conclusion is logical

**Elaboration**
___ uses interesting examples and details
___ uses adjectives and adverbs to enhance descriptions
___ expresses personal thoughts/feelings
___ word choice is accurate/vivid
___ uses descriptive phrases and clauses
___ includes analogies

**Structure and Writing Mechanics**
___ uses varying patterns and sentence length
___ includes simple, compound, and complex sentence structure
___ uses paragraphing appropriately (2+ sentences with topic sentence)
___ includes transition words smoothly to link sentences/paragraphs
___ uses subject/verb agreement in sentences
___ uses correct capitalization and punctuation
___ spells words correctly

**SCORE** _____ / __24__

# Holistic Rubric of Expository Written Language

**Student:** _____ **Grade:** _____

**Date:** _____ **Teacher:** _____

## Procedure:

Determine which descriptors and corresponding heading best applies to your student's work. Your student's score is 0, 1, 2, or 3.

**Score: 3**      **Meets Expectations**

Work is focused and fully developed without irrelevant information.

Ideas are sequenced and appropriately supported.

Effective transitions are used throughout.

Correct grammar, capitalization, and spelling are used throughout.

**Score: 2**      **Adequate**

There are minimal distractions in flow of thought.

Some support is provided for ideas, but they are not clearly explained.

Basic transitions are used.

There are some errors in mechanics (grammar, capitalization, spelling)

**Score: 1**      **Needs Improvement**

There are numerous distractions in flow of thought.

The format is rambling and poorly organized.

Support is insufficient, irrelevant, or ambiguous.

Transitions are inadequate.

There are numerous errors in mechanics.

**Score: 0**      **Inadequate**

There appears to be no organization of thought or content.

Sentences are difficult to read and understand.

**Student Score:** _____

# Intervention Progress Sheet

**Student:** _____ **Grade:** _____

**Teacher:** _____ Case Partner _____

Intervention(s)

Baseline

100%
90%
80%
70%
60%
50%
40%
30%
20%
10%
0%

**Dates**

**Definition of the Problem:** _____

**Objective:** _____

**Intervention:** _____

# Intervention Strategies Menu

Student: _____  Grade: _____

Date: _____  Teacher: _____

Below are successful alternative teaching strategies. Please check those you have used.

## Behavior

**To improve ability to attend to verbal information:**
- [ ] shortened length of listening activities
- [ ] reduced visual distractions in classroom
- [ ] provided pictures or other visual cues
- [ ] wrote key vocabulary on the board
- [ ] used taped material presented through headphones
- [ ] used choral speaking in group to maintain attention
- [ ] provided opportunities for periodic rehearsal of information presented verbally
- [ ] provided scribe for classroom notes; allowed student to copy notes from peer
- [ ] use graphic organizers
- [ ] decreased amount of visual distractions in the room
- [ ] scheduled class when student is more alert
- [ ] break longer presentations into shorter units
- [ ] allowed student to tape lesson
- [ ] touched or cued student when attention waned
- [ ] re-directed student when attention waned
- [ ] changed student's seat to decrease distractions
- [ ] shortened tasks and amount of material
- [ ] used material on student's instructional level

**To improve work completion:**
- [ ] used student checklist for work completion
- [ ] used study carrel
- [ ] used timer for work completion
- [ ] used headsets to block extraneous noise
- [ ] used stickers or token reinforcement system
- [ ] provided work one paper at a time
- [ ] used work assignment lists
- [ ] broke lengthy assignments into smaller parts
- [ ] reduced amount of written work
- [ ] simplified worksheets
- [ ] sent home extra set of texts

**To improve transitions between activities:**
- [ ] kept routine structured
- [ ] posted expected behavior & rules
- [ ] marked student's "space" & materials
- [ ] posted schedule of the day for transitions
- [ ] cued student prior to transition
- [ ] allowed student opportunities for movement

**To improve positive group participation skills:**
- [ ] praised positive participation
- [ ] called on student to share experiences/thoughts
- [ ] allowed rehearsal opportunities
- [ ] used role playing to teach appropriate behavior
- [ ] provided a "cool down" space
- [ ] provided older student or adult mentor
- [ ] used peer "buddy" to model appropriate behavior
- [ ] used time out procedure for acting out or aggressive behaviors
- [ ] used a written behavior contract with student
- [ ] used regular feedback between home & school

## Reading

**To improve decoding (word attack) skills:**
- [ ] checked on vision
- [ ] presented phonemic awareness activities
- [ ] used rhyming activities
- [ ] multi-sensory or VAKT = Visual-Auditory-Kinesthetic/Tactile instruction
- [ ] used color cues for sound blending (left to right)
- [ ] used fingers/markers for tracking left to right
- [ ] presented syllabication rules
- [ ] synthesized words (part to whole)
- [ ] segmented words (whole to part)
- [ ] changed to different reading series
- [ ] used word families
- [ ] provided opportunities for daily reading
- [ ] repeated phonic rules verbally (auditory cues)
- [ ] presented phonic rules on chart (visual cues)
- [ ] used log of misread words for practice
- [ ] used literature-based instruction with semantic cues
- [ ] small group instruction ___ daily
- [ ] 2-3 times/week ___ weekly
- [ ] sent home word list for home practices
- [ ] used guided reading group

**To improve sight word recognition skills:**
- [ ] used card reader/language master for drill/practice
- [ ] used word configuration cues
- [ ] sent word list home for home practice
- [ ] provided flash card practice
- [ ] used language experience/concrete meaning
- [ ] used a word wall for important vocabulary

**To improve reading comprehension skills:**
- [ ] pre-read story to student
- [ ] re-read favorite stories
- [ ] read stories with predictable text
- [ ] discussed pictures/illustrations before reading story (visual cues)
- [ ] asked student to answer questions orally first
- [ ] asked student to illustrate sentences or stories
- [ ] highlighted key concepts in text
- [ ] asked student to write sentences for reading vocabulary words
- [ ] asked student to list details of story
- [ ] used sequence pictures & then re-told story
- [ ] asked student to complete close sentences/paragraphs
- [ ] asked student to finish incomplete story
- [ ] used guided reading group
- [ ] used supplemental materials/resources
- [ ] used high interest texts at instructional level

## Listening

**To improve ability to follow verbal directions:**

- ☐ checked on hearing
- ☐ repeated directions ___ once ___ twice ___ three or more times
- ☐ rephrased directions
- ☐ provide preferential seating away from distracting noises (e.g., pencil sharperner)
- ☐ provide preferential seating near teacher or source of sound
- ☐ asked student to repeat directions
- ☐ simplified directions into one step at a time
- ☐ used visual cues or written directions paired with verbal directions
- ☐ used visual or auditory cue prior to giving directions
- ☐ presented directions at slower pace
- ☐ encouraged student to indicate when he/she doesn't understand
- ☐ avoided light behind my face (or window) when giving directions
- ☐ kept hands & objects away from my face when giving directions
- ☐ attained eye contact of student before giving directions
- ☐ assigned peer "buddy" to help student with directions
- ☐ presented directions in "routine" in the same manner & at the same time
- ☐ provided "wait" time to respond to directions

## Communication

**To improve vocabulary comprehension:**

- ☐ used real objects or materials when introducing vocabulary
- ☐ used photographs to illustrate new words/vocabulary
- ☐ developed "pictionary" for new words/vocabulary
- ☐ used hands-on experiences to teach new words/vocabulary
- ☐ taught new words/vocabulary in categories with association cues
- ☐ used mnemonic devices
- ☐ used word webbing activities
- ☐ pre-taught student on target words/vocabulary

**To improve expression language skills:**

- ☐ allowed "wait time" for verbal responses
- ☐ provided verbal cues or reminders to elicit correct language
- ☐ used choral speaking techniques with entire class or group
- ☐ asked student to imitate teacher's model
- ☐ used visual or written cues to elicit correct language
- ☐ used role playing activities
- ☐ modeled correct language or provided expanded form as model

**To improve articulation or speech skills:**

- ☐ modeled correct speech for student
- ☐ reminded student with verbal cues
- ☐ used non-verbal signal as a reminder
- ☐ provided praise or positive reinforcement for "good speech"
- ☐ practiced correct sound production using reading, spelling, or vocabulary lists

**To improve handwriting or written expression:**

- ☐ provided hand strengthening activities (e.g., clay, squeeze ball)
- ☐ provided special paper (e.g., raised lines, graph paper, unlined)
- ☐ used pencil grip
- ☐ used dark, bright, or high contrast written cues on paper
- ☐ used various writing tools (e.g., chalk, marker, crayon, erasable pen, etc.)
- ☐ used tracing paper for shape, letter, and number formation
- ☐ provided alphabet and number strips on desk
- ☐ used templates for shape, letter and number formation
- ☐ used multisensory activities, including sandpaper, sand, foam, salt, etc.
- ☐ used cues (e.g., finger space) for spacing between words
- ☐ seated student near blackboard for copying
- ☐ reduced copying from book or blackboard
- ☐ reduced amount of required written responses
- ☐ taught cursive writing as alternative to printing (manuscript)
- ☐ assigned a peer "writer" for copying
- ☐ assigned peer to transcribe written work or responses
- ☐ allowed student to tape record responses
- ☐ allowed use of spell checker
- ☐ taught keyboarding skills for typewriter or computer
- ☐ allowed "sloppy copy" for first draft
- ☐ used penmanship drill and practice
- ☐ used story starters or prompts
- ☐ used sequence stories for writing simple stories
- ☐ used rubric or checklist for proofing written work
- ☐ used graphic organizers
- ☐ allowed untimed written exams

## Mathematics

- ☐ reduced copying from book by using preprinted or copied sheets
- ☐ used legible, uncrowded worksheets
- ☐ used graph paper
- ☐ used flash cards for drill on facts
- ☐ used manipulatives
- ☐ provided repetition of math drills
- ☐ used songs, rhymes, or games
- ☐ allowed student to vocalize to self
- ☐ used number lines, counters, charts
- ☐ allowed student to use math facts table
- ☐ allowed student to use calculator
- ☐ reduced number of math examples
- ☐ highlighted key words in math problems

## Spelling

- ☐ used multisensory techniques (VAKT)
- ☐ used spelling flash cards for practice
- ☐ allowed student to spell into tape recorder
- ☐ used picture or color cues or word shapes
- ☐ taught sight words in a meaningful phrase or sentence
- ☐ taught specific spelling rules
- ☐ used same words for reading, spelling, and writing tasks
- ☐ tested only word lists, not sentences
- ☐ reduced number of expected words
- ☐ tested student orally
- ☐ sent home spelling words for practice

# Observable Positive and Negative Behaviors Chart

## Attention and Organization Skills

| Negative Behaviors | Positive Behaviors |
| --- | --- |
| Moves about or leaves classroom | Stays in assigned area |
| Doesn't follow verbal directions | Responds to verbal directions |
| Forgets or has difficulty transferring information | Uses learned information in a different setting |
| Doesn't pay attention | Visually attends to speaker |
| Perseverates or has difficulty with transitions | Moves smoothly from one activity to the next |
| Is distracted by sounds or people in the immediate area | Maintains attention to task |
| Loses possessions or has a messy work area | Shows responsibility for personal property |

## Group and Social Relationship Skills

| Negative Behaviors | Positive Behaviors |
| --- | --- |
| Acts out when others receive praise or attention | Follows classroom rules to gain praise or recognition |
| Is physically aggressive with adults or peers | Refrains from physically hurting others |
| Calls out in group or class discussions | Raises hand and responds when called on |
| Makes noises or inappropriate comments | Listens and responds appropriately |
| Makes profane comments to teachers | Speaks in a respectful manner |
| Doesn't share materials or space with others | Works cooperatively with other students |
| Destroys or steals others' possessions | Asks permission to touch others' possessions |
| Touches others inappropriately | Keeps hands away from others |

## Mood and Motivation

| Negative Behaviors | Positive Behaviors |
| --- | --- |
| Refuses to follow directions | Complies with teacher requests |
| Is tardy or absent from school or class without an acceptable excuse | Regularly attends class on time |
| Becomes easily upset by constructive criticism | Responds positively to teacher suggestions |
| Whines, cries, or has temper tantrums | Remains positively engaged in activity |
| Hurts himself or destroys his possessions | Improves his appearance or expresses positive feelings about himself |
| Hands in incomplete assignments or messy work with careless errors | Completes assignments accurately within designated time period |
| Copies or seeks inordinate amounts of assistance to complete work | Completes assignments independently |

# Behavior Observation Form

Student: _____   Observer Date:_____

Observation Date:_____   Time:_____

Class Activity: _____

| ANTECEDENT | BEHAVIOR | CONSEQUENCE |
|---|---|---|
| What happens before the behavior | What specific action student takes | What happens after the behavior |
|  |  |  |
|  |  |  |
|  |  |  |
|  |  |  |
|  |  |  |
|  |  |  |

# Behavior Observation Tally Sheet

Student:_____Observer: _____

Date of Observation:_____Setting & Activity: _____

Target Behavior: _____

Type of Measurement: _____ Frequency _____ Duration _____ Interval

| START TIME | STOP TIME | TALLY OR INTERVALS | | | | | | | | | | TOTAL |
|---|---|---|---|---|---|---|---|---|---|---|---|---|
| | | 1 | 2 | 3 | 4 | 5 | 6 | 7 | 8 | 9 | 10 | |
| | | | | | | | | | | | | |
| | | | | | | | | | | | | |
| | | | | | | | | | | | | |
| | | | | | | | | | | | | |
| | | | | | | | | | | | | |
| | | | | | | | | | | | | |
| | | | | | | | | | | | | |
| | | | | | | | | | | | | |
| | | | | | | | | | | | | |
| | | | | | | | | | | | | |

Behavior count:_____ Average duration:_____ Percentage: _____

Additional observations or comments: _____

_____

_____

_____

# Behavior Intervention Plan

**Student:** _____ **Date:** _____

**Grade:** _____ **Teacher:** _____

## Results of Functional Behavioral Assessment

| ANTECEDENTS | SPECIFIC BEHAVIOR | CONSEQUENCES | FUNCTION |
|---|---|---|---|
| | | | ☐ Gains peer attention<br>☐ Gains teacher attention<br>☐ Gains approval<br>☐ Gains item/material<br>☐ Avoids task<br>☐ Avoids stimulation<br>☐ Avoids individual(s)<br>☐ Other<br>_____ |

Frequency of occurrence: ____(number) incidents per ____ hour, ____ day, ____ week, ____ month

Duration of occurrence: From ____ (circle time) minutes or hours    to ____ minutes or hours

**Interventions used to date:**

_____   Effective ____   Ineffective ____

_____   Effective ____   Ineffective ____

_____   Effective ____   Ineffective ____

_____   Effective ____   Ineffective ____

## Intervention Plan

**Desired Behavior:** _____

| INTERVENTION(S) | LOCATION | REINFORCER(S) | PERSON(S) RESPONSIBLE |
|---|---|---|---|
| | | | |

**Process to Monitor Intervention:** How Often: ____ Daily ____ Weekly ____ Monthly

Monitoring Method: ____ Formal Observation ____ Student Conference ____ Parent Conference

**Evidence of Accomplishment:** _____

# Possible Data Collection Methods

| BEHAVIORS | TYPE OF DATA COLLECTION |
|---|---|

**Behaviors that last for a period of time, for example:**

- ☐ being out of seat for a time period
- ☐ crying
- ☐ daydreaming
- ☐ perseverating on a behavior
- ☐ playing with items in desk
- ☐ attending to speaker

### Duration

**What to record:** Note when the behavior begins and when it ends.

**What to use:** Stop watch, clock, video tape, egg timer

---

**Behaviors that occur as separate or recurring events, for example:**

- ☐ getting in and out of seat
- ☐ hitting or touching others
- ☐ losing or taking others' possessions
- ☐ making noises
- ☐ raising hand
- ☐ asking to leave the room
- ☐ talking back to teacher
- ☐ being tardy for class
- ☐ using profanity
- ☐ yelling out in class or verbal outbursts
- ☐ temper tantrums
- ☐ completing work

### Frequency

**What to record:** Record each time the behavior occurs as a tally during a set time period.

**What to use:** Pennies or tokens moved from pocket to pocket; chips or tokens put in a container; stickers, happy faces, or stars put on charts.

---

**Behaviors that are inconsistently or not easily observed, for example:**

- ☐ attending to task or attending to distractions
- ☐ refusing to follow directions
- ☐ talking in class
- ☐ whining
- ☐ moving smoothly between activities

### Interval

**What to record:** Select a length of time (e.g., one minute). Observe the student at each interval and note "+" if the behavior is present or "–" if the behavior is not present.

**What to use:** Marks on masking tape on wrist; checks on post-it notes, mailing labels, or index cards.

# Sequence-of-the-Day Planning Sheet

Student: _____  Grade: _____

Date: _____  Teacher _____

| SEQUENCE OF THE DAY | IEP GOALS, OBJECTIVES, AND BENCHMARKS | | | | | | |
|---|---|---|---|---|---|---|---|
| | | | | | | | |
| | | | | | | | |
| | | | | | | | |
| | | | | | | | |
| | | | | | | | |
| | | | | | | | |
| | | | | | | | |

# Team Teaching/Co-Teaching Daily Lesson Plan

Class/Subject: _____

General Classroom Teacher: _____     Special Education Staff: _____

| Date | What are you going to teach (content)? | How will the class be grouped? | What are the key points of the lesson? | What materials are needed? | Which students need accommodations? | How will you evaluate learning (product)? |
|------|------|------|------|------|------|------|
|      |      |      |      |      |      |      |
|      |      |      |      |      |      |      |
|      |      |      |      |      |      |      |
|      |      |      |      |      |      |      |

# Special Area Class Communication Form

**Student:** _____     **To:   Art:** _____

**Date:** _____     **Music:** _____

**From:** _____ **IEP Team**     **P.E.:** _____

_____ **Early Intervention Team**     **Media:** _____

A meeting will be held to discuss the progress and current performance of the student listed above on _____ at _____.

We would appreciate any pertinent information about this student's academic performance, behavior, and work completion that you have seen in your classroom.

**Current performance:** _____ above grade level expectations

_____ adequate; at grade level

_____ below grade level expectations

Other:_____

**Behavior:**    attends to instruction    ___ Yes    ___ No

follows directions/rules    ___ Yes    ___ No

participates in class    ___ Yes    ___ No

volunteers in class    ___ Yes    ___ No

Other: _____

**Work Completion:** _____ completes assignments on time

_____ assignments are missing or incomplete

Other: _____

Other comments: _____

_____

_____

Please return this form to _____ by (date) _____

Thank you for your assistance.

# Sample Format for Writing Goals, Objectives, and Benchmarks

**Consider the formula below for writing goals, objectives, and benchmarks for your student:**

**Condition + Accommodation + Student's Name + Skill/Task/Behavior + Performance Criteria**

## Example A

Given at least five opportunities during classroom discussions to ask questions and make comments, and one verbal prompt from the teacher, Dan will raise his hand and respond when acknowledged with 90 percent accuracy on three consecutive days.

## Example B

By June, when given a fourth grade level writing prompt and extended time, Chris will compose a written response of at least three paragraphs expressing clear meaning, internal structure, organization, correct syntax, and spelling with 90% accuracy on three consecutive weekly assignments.

## Examples of Conditions

- Given a random selection of 20 words from a pool of 100 words
- Given a fourth grade reading passage
- Given a worksheet of 10 examples/problems
- Given five opportunities to do X (a specific task)
- Given the weekly spelling test
- Given an end-of-term multiple choice test format/true-false test format
- Given a sixth grade level writing prompt
- Given a group activity of 20 minutes
- Given the classroom setting

## Examples of Accommodations

- Braillewriter
- Signed translation
- Communication device
- Picture exchange board
- Scanner
- Reader
- Large print display
- Slant board
- Calculator
- Spell checker
- Repeated instructions
- Audiotape recorded instructions
- Highlighted key words in a written passage
- Colored acetate
- Visual, verbal, physical prompting
- Extended time
- Individual carrel

# 100 Active Verbs for Writing Goals, Objectives, and Benchmarks

Here are 100 active verbs you can use to write observable and measurable student expectations (e.g., target behaviors, goals, objectives, benchmarks).

| | | |
|---|---|---|
| add | diagram | operate |
| analyze | differentiate | organize |
| apply | differentiate between | pick |
| appraise | discriminate | plan |
| arrange | discuss | predict |
| assemble | distinguish | prepare |
| calculate | divide | present |
| categorize | dramatize | produce |
| choose | draw conclusions | propose |
| cite examples of | employ | question |
| collect | engage in | read |
| communicate | estimate | recall |
| compare | evaluate | recognize |
| complete | examine | reconstruct |
| compose | experiment | record |
| conclude | explain | relate |
| construct | express | repeat |
| contrast | follow directions | report |
| correlate | formulate | respond |
| copy | identify | restate |
| create | illustrate | review |
| criticize | imitate | select |
| debate | infer | sequence |
| deduce | initiate | solve |
| define | inspect | spell |
| demonstrate | interact | state |
| demonstrate use of | interpret | subtract |
| describe | list | tell |
| design | locate | translate |
| detect | manage | underline |
| determine | modify | use |
| develop | multiply | utilize |
| devise | name | write |
| diagnose | | |

# Accommodations and Modifications
# Planning Worksheet

Student: _____ Grade: _____

Date: _____ Teacher: _____

| Time | Activity and Accommodation or Modification | Level of Participation | Implementer(s) |
|------|--------------------------------------------|------------------------|----------------|
|      |                                            |                        |                |
|      |                                            |                        |                |
|      |                                            |                        |                |
|      |                                            |                        |                |

Note: Level of Participation  P = Partial;  F = Full

# Accommodations and Modifications Checklist

The accommodations and modifications checked below are required for the following student.

Student: _____  Grade: _____

Date: _____  Teacher: _____

## ENVIRONMENT OR SETTING
- ☐ Seat near teacher
- ☐ Assign student to low-distraction area
- ☐ Seat near positive peer models
- ☐ Use study carrel
- ☐ Use of time-out
- ☐ Define physical space for student within the room
- ☐ Stand near student when giving instructions
- ☐ Display specific behavioral rules
- ☐ Special lighting

## PRESENTATION
- ☐ Use visual aids with oral presentation
- ☐ Display key vocabulary
- ☐ Use multisensory presentation
- ☐ Use concrete or personalized examples
- ☐ Provide models
- ☐ Course outlines or study guides
- ☐ Highlight instructions (marker or highlighter tape)
- ☐ Use markers or organizers to keep place
- ☐ Repeat directions
- ☐ Student to repeat instructions for comprehension
- ☐ Use mnemonics
- ☐ Provide student with vocabulary word bank
- ☐ Use motivational game-like materials
- ☐ Call on student often
- ☐ Acknowledge effort
- ☐ Prompt student to stay on task
- ☐ Provide additional prompts & cues as needed
- ☐ Use dark ink or raised lines
- ☐ Use increased spacing between items on page
- ☐ Use buff-colored rather than white paper
- ☐ Provide prompts on audiotape
- ☐ Allow student to tape-record lesson
- ☐ Arrange for a note taker
- ☐ Use sign language interpreter
- ☐ Give student a copy of lecture notes

## PACE, TIME, OR SCHEDULING
- ☐ Permit breaks between tasks
- ☐ Provide "wait" time for responses
- ☐ Display daily schedule
- ☐ Modify student's schedule to fit optimal learning times

## CURRICULUM CONTENT
- ☐ Adjust work load
- ☐ Reduce assignments
- ☐ Simplify number of items presented on page
- ☐ Give alternative assignments in subject
- ☐ Pre-teach content

## RESPONSE MODE
- ☐ Allow oral responses
- ☐ Permit scribe for answers
- ☐ Use pencil grip
- ☐ Use calculator, math tables, or abacus
- ☐ Use spell checker or dictionary
- ☐ Use tape recorder
- ☐ Allow alternate response mode: _____
  (e.g., Braille, picture exchange system, sign language)

## ADAPTED MATERIALS OR EQUIPMENT
- ☐ Use large type/magnifying equipment
- ☐ Keep page format simple
- ☐ Divide page into clearly marked sections
- ☐ Remove distractions from paper
- ☐ Use slant board or wedge
- ☐ Use computer-assisted instruction
- ☐ Use adapted equipment: _____
  (e.g., adapted computer keyboard, communication device, Braillewriter)

## ORGANIZATIONAL STRATEGIES
- ☐ Training in how to take notes
- ☐ Give one assignment at a time
- ☐ Checklist on desk for work completed
- ☐ Folders to hold work
- ☐ Post assignments
- ☐ Use calendar to plan long-term assignments
- ☐ Use of assignment notebook
- ☐ Give time to organize desk during class
- ☐ AM check-in to organize for the day
- ☐ Lunch time check-in to organize for PM
- ☐ PM check-out to organize for homework
- ☐ Assign homework partner
- ☐ Arrange for duplicate materials to use at home
- ☐ Develop parent/school contract
- ☐ Provide training in time management

## TYPE OF INSTRUCTION
- ☐ Individual or small group instruction
- ☐ Peer tutoring
- ☐ Cross-age tutoring
- ☐ Study-buddy
- ☐ Work with paraeducator
- ☐ Confer with staff during available times
- ☐ Teach student to monitor own behavior
- ☐ Implement behavior contract & reward system
- ☐ Conflict resolution strategies
- ☐ Other: _____

# Accommodations and Modifications
## Assessment Checklist

The accommodations and modifications checked below are required for the following student.

**Student:** _____  **Grade:** _____

**Date:** _____  **Teacher:** _____

### ASSESSMENT ACCOMMODATIONS OR MODIFICATIONS

- ☐ Use short, frequent quizzes
- ☐ Permit breaks during tests
- ☐ Permit movement
- ☐ Reduce number of test items
- ☐ Limit multiple choice
- ☐ Preview test procedures
- ☐ Practice taking similar test questions
- ☐ Periodic checks for answers marked in correct spaces
- ☐ Arrange for oral testing
- ☐ Support staff administers test
- ☐ Permit student to type or use word processing
- ☐ Permit untimed testing
- ☐ Give test over several sessions
- ☐ Administer test at specific time of day
- ☐ Administer test in separate setting
- ☐ Administer using a study carrel
- ☐ Give prior notice for quizzes
- ☐ Read test to student
- ☐ Permit templates to reduce visible print
- ☐ Rephrase test questions and directions
- ☐ Allow open book or notes
- ☐ Increase size of bubbles on answer sheet
- ☐ Provide cues on answer sheet
- ☐ Secure answer sheet to work area
- ☐ Student marks on test booklet
- ☐ Permit adapted format: _____
- ☐ Use adapted equipment: _____

### GRADING
- ☐ Use grading criteria based on individual ability
- ☐ Base grade on IEP
- ☐ Adjusted grading option; grade satisfactory/unsatisfactory, credit/no credit
- ☐ No spelling penalty
- ☐ No handwriting penalty

# Conference Planning Sheet for Parents

A conference with your child's teacher is scheduled for _____ at _____ in room _____.
This planning sheet will help you think about what you may want to discuss during the conference. Please bring it to the conference with you.

1) **Talk to your child before the conference.** Explain that you are going to be meeting with his or her teacher. Tell your child you want to help the teacher as much as you can. Find out what his or her best subjects are and which subjects he or she likes the least. Ask why certain subjects are easier than others. Also, ask your child if there is anything you should talk about with his or her teacher(s).
   - What questions or concerns does your child have about school? (Complete this section with your child.)

2) **To help you prepare, think about the following questions before you come to the conference.**
   - What are my goals for my child this year?
   - Is my child dealing with any health problems or family situations that could affect his or her behavior or academic progress?
   - What do I want the teacher to know about my child. (for example, personality, habits, hobbies)?

3) **To use the conference time efficiently, write down any questions you have for your child's teacher(s) about the curriculum or classroom expectations.**
   For example:
   - What skills and knowledge is my child expected to master this year?
   - How will my child be evaluated? What kinds of tests will he or she take?
   - How well does my child get along with others?
   - Is my child working up to his or her ability?
   - Has my child missed any classes? Does he or she hand in homework on time?
   - Does my child participate in class discussions?
   - What type of special help is available to help my child progress?
   - Other questions: _____

4) **Children do better in school when their parents are actively involved in their education. Before you leave the conference, ask this question:**
   - How can I help my child do better in school?

# Weekly Homework Log

Student: _____ Grade: _____

Week of: _____ Teacher: _____

| Subject | Monday | Tuesday | Wednesday | Thursday | Friday |
|---------|--------|---------|-----------|----------|--------|
|         |        |         |           |          |        |
|         |        |         |           |          |        |
|         |        |         |           |          |        |
|         |        |         |           |          |        |
|         |        |         |           |          |        |
|         |        |         |           |          |        |
|         |        |         |           |          |        |
|         |        |         |           |          |        |
| Materials Needed |  |    |           |          |        |

Parent Signature: _____ Date: _____

# Daily Home Report

Student: _____ Grade: _____

Date: _____ Teacher: _____

I am working on: (goal) _____

Today, I:

|  | not at all | sometimes | most of the time |
|---|:---:|:---:|:---:|
| Followed directions | 1 | 2 | 3 |
| Completed my work in class | 1 | 2 | 3 |
| Followed classroom rules | 1 | 2 | 3 |
| Kept my work space neat | 1 | 2 | 3 |
| Got along well with others | 1 | 2 | 3 |

Teachers Comments: _____

_____

___ Signature: _____

Parent's Comments: _____

_____

___ Signature: _____

# Toolkit Notes